The Insider's Guide to Hawaii Volcanoes National Park

The Best Things to See and Do at Kilauea Volcano, Including Volcano Village

Newly Revised 2016 Edition

By Uldra Johnson

*****

Aloha, e komo mai! Welcome!

So you're planning a visit to the land of the most active volcano on planet Earth and the most sacred site in Hawaii!

You will be one of more than 2.5 million people from all over the globe who visits the Big Island each year to witness Earth-in-the-making, an experience that you will never forget!

Molten and congealed lava flows, huge, moonlike, steaming calderas, prehistoric lava tube caves, toxic steam clouds lifting hundreds of feet into the blue tropical skies, and lava tree molds are set within the pristine, emerald jewel of a rainforest, where rare songbirds and exotic plants that occur no where else on the planet thrive in a virtual Garden of Eden.

Sound exciting?

It is!

Designated an International Biosphere Reserve and a World Heritage Site, the Park, as we locals call it, is also considered by scientists to be the most ideal living laboratory in the world for the study of ecology and geology.

Why?

Because the Hawaiian Islands are the most geographically isolated islands on earth, and yet this ecological and geographical wonderland is so accessible.

I explore almost daily the many wonders of the Park, on my own as a naturalist and photographer, and as a professional tour guide. I never tire of the incredible beauty of the delicate rainforest and the awesome power of the Kilauea Volcano. I love Kilauea, and I truly enjoy sharing this precious natural treasure with others.

This guide will take you to my favorite places, tell you where to go, what to look for, and what to take for comfort and safety. You can choose from scenic car stops that overlook steaming calderas or black, frozen lava flows as far as the eye can see, and satisfy your desire for a few moments of eye-candy and photograph-taking, to isolated, rugged camping trails that test your psychological and physical endurance.

Want to sit hidden away beneath the world's tallest ferns in a natural grotto, listen to the exotic songs of forest birds, and meditate? Or perhaps you feel like exploring among the crystal and rainbow titanium lava shards on the still-steaming floor of a caldera, while rare Hawaiian hawks soar high above your head?

Maybe you'd like to spend a day wandering and wondering among the more than 20,000 mysterious, ancient petroglyphs carved in an ancient lava flow, each with an enigmatic story to tell?

Then again, you might be the kind to enjoy spelunking through a secreted lava cave with gold and silver icicle-shaped lava stalactites hanging from the roof. It's all here! And much more!

Many visitors to the Park come on the great big busses which virtually whiz through in a few hours, stopping for mere moments at a few convenient places marked "busses only," but if you're reading this guide, you probably are planning a longer, more personalized, more rewarding trip to the Volcano. Perhaps you are planning to spend more than a day exploring the Park, and I certainly suggest that you do! In that case, you probably will plan to stay in nearby magical Volcano Village, famous for its artists.

Almost everyone in the Village is an artist; if not an artist, they probably work in the Park. If not that, they probably run a Bed-and-Breakfast or vacation rental; there are almost two hundred in a storybook village with the population of only 2231! One thing is for sure, everyone who lives here loves it and appreciates and protects this very special and sacred environment. For you folks who would like to share in the flavor of the Village, if for a day or longer, you will find here wonderful tidbits of information to make your visit forever memorable.

My Favorite Places

Here it is—a list of my favorite places! This guide will take you to all these extraordinary places, and more.

Ainahou Ranch
Chain of Craters
Devastation Trail and Desolation Peak
Halema'uma'u Crater
Hilina Pali Trail

Holei Sea Arch
Jaggar Museum and Halema'uma'u Crater
Ka'u Desert Footprints
Kilauea Caldera
Kilauea I'ki Caldera Overlook and Trail
Kipuka Puaulu (Bird Park)
Mauna Ulu (Growing Mountain)
Nahuku Crater and Thurston Lava Tube
Namakani Paio (The Conflicting Winds)
Kilauea Overlook and Uwekahuna Bluff
Napau Trail (The Endings)
'Ola'a Rainforest
Place of the Guardians (Pele's Playground)
Pu'u Huluhulu (Shaggy Hill)
Pua Po'o (Cock's Comb Cave, Wild Cave)
Puu Loa Petroglyphs
Steaming Bluff
Sulfur Banks
Sandalwood Trail
The Enchanted Forest
The Strip
Tree Molds
Volcano Art Gallery

Are you ready? Let's begin with a quick overview of geology, ecology, flora, fauna and Hawaiian culture of this fabulous place.

*****

Geology

Everyone is interested in geology these days. Why?

Even many scientists are wondering if we're going toward a new period of increased volcanic explosions and earthquakes. Millions of people even believe that increased volcanic activity is a sign of the end of the world, the Second Coming, impending visitations by extra-terrestrials, or earth changes as predicted by the Mayan calendar!

At any rate, volcanoes are currently active in Italy, Russia, Chile, Ecuador, New Britain, Indonesia, Costa Rica, Santa Maria, Guatemala, and Indonesia, as well as in Hawaii. There has been growing concern about the huge "super volcano" in Yellowstone National Park.

Some scientists predict that, in the case of simultaneous major eruptions within a short period of time, it's possible that the Earth would be cooled by at least one to three degrees, as all the dust and ash in the upper atmosphere would partly shield the sun's rays and greatly disturb worldwide weather patterns. Earthquakes and volcanoes are related to the movement of the Earth's plates, called plate tectonics, causing changes in density and pressure, which are correlated to volcanic activity. Large earthquakes can trigger volcanic eruptions, and magma movement can cause tremors.

Recent natural disasters, such as the huge earthquake and tsunami in Japan, have impressed everyone that Earth changes affect us all. And the magnitude of these disasters has reminded us that humans are powerless when confronted by these colossal forces of Mother Nature. These huge geological events have made us curious about our planet again.

Hawaii Volcanoes National Park offers the visitor a look at two of the world's most active volcanoes: Kilauea and Mauna Loa.

More than 4,000 feet high and still growing, Kilauea abuts the southeastern slope of the older and much larger Mauna Loa, or "Long Mountain." Mauna Loa towers some 13,679 feet above the sea, making it the tallest mountain in the world, and the second tallest in the solar system (Mars has the honor of the highest mountain). Yes, it's true. Measured from its base 18,000 feet below sea level, Mauna Loa exceeds Mount Everest in height.

Hawaii Volcanoes National Park stretches from sea level to Mauna Loa's summit. Seven ecological zones exist within Hawaii Volcanoes National Park. Each zone consists of distinct plant and animal communities. Kilauea's caldera is surrounded by three zones: rain forest on the east, upland forests and woodlands on the northwest, and mid-elevation woodlands to the south.

Beyond the end of the road to Mauna Loa lies Mauna Loa's wilderness area, where hikers encounter freezing nights and jagged lava trails amid volcanic wonders: stark lava twisted into black licorice shapes, cinder cones, gaping pits.

Kilauea, however, provides easy access to a greater variety of scenery and cultural sites. In fact, it is often called the "drive-in" volcano. On the slopes of Kilauea, whose name means "much spewing," lush green rain forests border barren, recent lava flows.

We're lucky!

Why?

Because for all its activity, and Kilauea has been continuously active now since 1983, Kilauea is a relatively "safe" volcano, at least as compared to other active volcanoes. Not that it hasn't created a path of devastation! It has destroyed more than 181 houses, a visitor center in the Park as well as important archeological sites, and its lava flows have enveloped roads and covered the famed Kalapana Black Sand Beach.

But it is considered "safe" and is the most visited volcano in the world because of the type of volcano it is; it is what is called a "shield" volcano. The Hawaiian Islands are all formed by shield volcanoes.

The form of a volcano is determined by the ingredients of the erupting magma. Their shapes are determined by the explosivity of the eruptions and the amount of water in the magma. Shield volcanoes are low and broad, with the entire summit region flattened or depressed. They have rift zones: two to four cracks radiating from the summit. Think *huge* cracks!

Shield volcanoes are almost exclusively basalt, a type of lava that is very fluid when erupted. For this reason, these volcanoes are not steep-sided, but shaped like a warrior's shield; hence the name. Eruptions at shield volcanoes are only explosive if water somehow gets into the vent; otherwise, they are characterized by low-explosive fountaining that forms cinder cones and spatter cones at the vent. Shield volcanoes are the result of high magma supply rates; the lava is hot and little changed from the time it was generated. Shield volcanoes are the common product of hotspot volcanism. More on hotspots in a moment.

On the other hand, subduction-zone strato volcanoes are tall and steep, with limited summit depression and no rift zones. Subduction-strato volcanoes comprise the largest percentage, almost 60%, of the Earth's volcanoes, and are characterized by eruptions of andesite and dacite—lavas that are cooler and more viscous than basalt. These more viscous lavas allow gas pressures to build up to high levels; these volcanoes are characterized by violent, explosive eruptions. The lava at strato volcanoes barely flows, instead piling up in the vent to form volcanic domes. The magma supply rates to strato volcanoes are lower. This is the cause of the cooler magma and the reason for the usually long repose periods between eruptions. Examples of strato volcanoes include Mt. St. Helens, Mt. Rainier, Pinatubo, Mt. Fuji, Merapi, Galeras, Cotopaxi, and others.

In other words, what this means is that, in general, shield volcanoes, not being accompanied by pyroclastic material, such as rocks and gasses of up to 1830 degrees Fahrenheit, moving at speeds of over 100-450 miles per hour, are relatively safe for us to explore!

This does not mean, however, that shield volcanoes never have explosive episodes. In fact, in 1959, Kilauea I 'ki caldera, one of the must-see sights on your visit, erupted violently in fountains 1900 feet tall! The good news is however, that it gave plenty of warning, preceding its violent outburst by swarms of earthquakes beginning three months in advance of its November 14th eruption.

Speaking of earthquakes, just to let you know, a number of earthquakes occur daily in the Kilauea area. Most of the time, these are below the threshold of perception. But, if you decide to spend a night in Volcano Village, and you are extremely sensitive, as I am, you may feel the earth trembling as you lay in bed at night. And if you are extremely sensitive, you may be interested to know that that faint rumble that you are not sure if you hear or feel, as you lie quietly in bed at night in the Village, may be coming from the roiling magma just one to four miles beneath the summit!

Though the chance of being caught in an explosive eruption in the Park is remote, there are very real dangers, and an entire section of this guide will be devoted to possible hazards and cautionary measures. But as I am writing now of fire and brimstone, this would be a good place to mention that, though Kilauea is often called the "drive-in" volcano, injuries and deaths do happen. In 1993, my good friend, photographer Prem Nagar, had a fiery death when a small earthquake caused the newly formed lava shelf on which he had ventured for up-close photos, to drop into the sea, heated beyond boiling by the river of molten lava flowing into it. He was never recovered. So, for the entire Park's beauty, please remember, you are not in Disneyland!

Pertinent geological facts relating to specific sites will be discussed below, but here is some more fascinating information relating to the way new earth is formed by the volcanoes here in Hawaii.

You may not know but the Hawaiian Islands are only part of a long continuous chain of islands that stretches northwest of Kauai 1900 miles to Midway Island and the Kure atoll and beyond. The Hawaiian Island chain is one of the largest and most striking features on the surface of planet Earth, yet it is not related to any of the major types of plate boundaries. The chain consists not only of the main Hawaiian Islands and adjacent French Frigate shoals, but also the Emperor Seamounts, a submarine range that runs northward to the Aleutian subduction zone where it disappears. This continuous line of volcanoes represents anomalous lava production and by implication, a zone of excess heat in the underlying mantle. In the early 1960's, the term "hotspot" was coined for regions like Hawaii where anomalous heat was recognized, though the origin of such regions remains a geological mystery.

What exactly is a hotspot? Think of a Krispy Kreme machine! Geologists believe that a huge column of upwelling lava, known as a "plume," lies at a fixed position under the Pacific Plate. As the ocean floor moves over this "hot spot" at about five inches a year, the upwelling lava creates a steady succession of new volcanoes that migrate along with the plate.

The Hawaiian-Emperor chain is the most famous and well studied of the hot spots that dot our planet. The youngest islands lie to the southeast, with the Big Island being the newest. The islands and seamounts become progressively older towards the northwest, bending sharply toward the north about halfway along its length. About 30-40 million years ago, something caused the direction of plate movement to change from almost due north to northwest, resulting in the Hawaii-Emperor Bend. A huge meteor strike, perhaps? No one knows.

The oldest seamounts are found at the northwest end of the trench, poised to plunge beneath the Aleutian volcanic arc. Picture a conveyor belt! The oldest volcanoes yet to be consumed are 70 million years old, having erupted at about the time that the last dinosaur died. Now these old volcanoes are dying. In other words, the hot spot has channeled magma up since at least the end of the dinosaur age. How many other volcanoes have already been subsumed we have no way of knowing.

The farther the other islands in the chain are from Hawaii, the greater their age. About 150 miles to the northwest is Oahu, which burst out of the sea about 3.5 million years ago. Midway, one of the oldest islands in the chain, was formed between 15 and 25 million years ago.

All in all, there are about 80 volcanoes from here to Alaska; that means on average about one volcano was made every one million years. As these volcanoes float off the hot spot, and move toward the Aleutians, they begin to sink. Why? Due to their weight, as well as factors of erosion by wind and water, gradually, as they age, where once they were mighty mountains, they become nothing more than coral reefs. They sink approximately 0.8 inches per 1000 years.

The Hawaiian archipelago consists of eight high islands, which means islands that have their highest elevation greater than a few hundred meters. These eight comprise 99% of the chain's emergent land area, land above the sea. These and the Northwestern Hawaiian Islands form a chain about 1500 miles long, with no continent closer than 2000 miles. It is the most isolated major group of islands on earth.

More about the mysterious hotspots. There are about 100 hotspots on the planet, but the total amount of lava produced by these is relatively slight, less than 1% of the volcanic material extruded worldwide. It has, interestingly, a different chemical composition than lava produced from the seafloor or subduction zones, the other two ways lava is produced. Hotspot magma is basalt. It contains less silicon as well as more iron and magnesium than does andesite. Andesite is continental igneous rock, containing high amounts of silicon, calcium, sodium and potassium, with low amounts of iron and magnesium.

To refresh your memory from fourth grade science, molten rock, when still under the Earth, is called magma. When it rises to the surface, it is called lava.

You may recall from your fourth grade science class that there are three layers of the Earth—the core, the mantle, and the crust. The core is the innermost portion, and is believed to be solid in the center and molten on its outer layer, with a temperature of up to 7000 Celsius. The mantle surrounds the core, heated to extremely high temperatures by the core. It is probably not liquid, but fluid enough to deform and flow very slowly. The crust is the very thin outer layer, consisting of the rigid rock of the seafloors and the continents.

Molten rock, magma, is somehow, not exactly known how, drawn or pushed up the hotspot to the surface, where it becomes a "seamount." As it grows and finally breaks the surface, it becomes an "island." The five volcanoes of the Big Island are sort of fused together to form what we call Hawaii Island.

These five connected volcanic mountains were built by a lava plume rising from the mantle. They are Mauna Loa, Kilauea, Mauna Kea, Hualalai, and Kohala. Kilauea, the world's largest active volcano, is still rumbling because the island has yet to drift completely off the hot spot.

Kohala is the oldest of Hawaii's subaerial volcanoes, about 430,000 years old. It is currently about 1670 meters above sea level, a loss of 1000 meters from its highest elevation, because it is already beginning to erode. It is considered extinct; it has not erupted for 60,000 years.

Mauna Kea is a dormant volcano and last erupted about 4500 years ago. It will probably erupt again some day. Interestingly, Mauna Kea is the only volcano in the Hawaiian chain known to have been glaciated. About 15,000 years ago, a glacier descended to about the 11,000 feet level and melted . Glacial ice resulted in a type of rock that was highly sought after by the ancient Hawaiians for adzes, because it is fine-grained and vesicle free, making it less likely to shatter. Mauna Loa was high enough to have had glaciers, but if glacial deposits formed, they have been buried by later flows.

Hualalai is the third most active volcano in Hawaii, and last erupted in 1801. It is expected to erupt again within the next 100 years.

Did you fly in via the Kona airport? That airport, and the surrounding real estate, some of the priciest in the world, are built upon that 1801 lava flow. Flows from Hualalai will reach the sea in less than a day. If and when Hualalai erupts again, there's a lot of Kailua-Kona in the way!

Mauna Loa, the largest mountain on earth, covers 51% of the Big Island. Since 1850, is has erupted on average every 7-10 years. It last erupted in 1984. You can see it is long overdue; it may erupt again at any time. Mauna Loa probably emerged from the sea 400,000 years, and has been erupting for 700,000 years.

Kilauea is the star, however. Beloved and feared as the home of the fire Goddess Pele, Halema'uma'u Crater, the center of Kilauea volcano, has been the source of countless Hawaiian legends. Kilauea, the youngster of the Hawaii volcanoes, first erupted between 300,000 and 600,000 years ago. That hotspot mentioned earlier is directly underneath Kilauea, perhaps as deep as 2000 miles into the mantle of the planet. The caldera was the site of nearly continuous activity during the 19th century and the early part of this century.

Since 1952, Kilauea has erupted 34 times, and since January 1983, eruptive activity has been continuous along the east rift zone. Currently, there is a lava lake within Halema'uma'u that rises and falls with the inflation and deflation of the lava beneath its summit, often exposing its red-hot interior. More on this later!

Note that in the paragraph about Kohala volcano the term subaerial volcano was used. That means a growing volcano has added enough mass and height to end frequent contact with water, thereby becoming less explosive.

There actually is an older volcano that formed Hawaii Island, Mahukona.

Mahukona is submerged on the northwestern flank of Island. Now it is a drowned coral reef at about 3,770 feet below sea level. A major break in slope at about 4,400 feet below sea level represents its old shorelines. The summit of this shield volcano was once 800 feet above sea level. The main shield-building stage of volcanism ended about 470,000 years ago. The summit subsided below sea level between 435,000 and 365,000 years ago. This makes Mahukona the granddaddy volcano of Hawaii Island.

And what's that about a baby volcano? Are we expecting?

Yes!

Though Kilauea is growing and will continue to grow throughout human history, it is not the baby volcano. That distinction goes to… Lo'ihi. Still technically a seamount rather than a volcano, Lo'ihi is the youngest volcano of the Hawaiian chain, lying about 35 km off the SE coast of the island of Hawaii. Nine hundred and fifty meters below sea level, this baby already has a caldera.

Lo'ihi began forming around 400,000 years ago, and will emerge above the sea about 10,000 to 100,000 years from now. It now stands more than

3,000 meters above the seafloor, making it taller than Mt. St. Helens before its 1980 eruption. If you're interested in buying prime ocean front real estate, for only $39.95, you can buy a parcel of Lo'ihi Seaview Estates now. Just Google it if you're interested!

We'll have more site-specific geology later on!

Ecology

Barren rocks in vast ocean waters, thousands of miles from the nearest land. How did the incredible diversity of life ever reach Hawaii shores?

Hawaii is 2551 miles from Los Angeles, 3850 miles from Japan, and 5280 miles from the Philippines, but insects and spiders and the seeds of plants reached the islands by wind or in the digestive tracts of birds or stuck to birds blown far off course. Sea currents carried salt-resistant seeds to these far shores, and perhaps some plants and animals floated here merely by chance, clinging to floating flotsam and jetsam.

Who can recount the heroic struggle of some desperate creature, hanging on for dear life?

What were the odds of life reaching these shores? And surviving?

It is estimated that a plant or animal colonized Hawaii at the rate of one every 70, 000 years. Over the past 70 million years, before the arrival of humans, few arrived; fewer survived.

The fortunate species that did make it to these islands evolved over time into new forms and species, and adapted to a life with an absence of predators and

18

competitors. Because of this, they no longer depended upon highly evolved defense mechanisms. Native plants evolved in the absence of mammalian plant eaters and lost ancestral defenses against predation such as thorny and poisonous foliage, bitter barks, and roots resistant to trampling. Plants did not need to evolve thorns or poisons for their protection; birds did not necessarily need wings!

More than 90% percent of the native flora and fauna of Hawaii is endemic,which means found nowhere else on our planet. From perhaps 20 original ancestors, the Island's 100 endemic birds evolved. Of Hawaii's native angiosperms (flowering plants) comprising some 1400 species, more than 96 percent are endemic, the rest are indigenous. Ten thousand spider and insect species evolved from 350 to 400 ancestors. Native ferns comprise about 170 species, with around 65 percent endemic. Mosses and liverworts are similar to ferns in these statistics. The Islands became home to only two endemic mammals, the Hawaiian monk seal and the hoary bat.

Most of these plants and animals lived together in a delicious harmony of co-existence, a Garden of Eden. There were no reptiles or amphibians. Hawaii was originally a paradise—no ants, mosquitoes, cockroaches, scorpions or large venomous centipedes. No snakes.

Where did these colonizers come from?

Only about 18% have affinities with North American species. The remainder came from Malaysia, Australia, New Zealand, southern South America and southeast Asia.

A Garden of Eden.

Then humans came. Predators.

The ancient Hawaiians brought a cornucopia of 26 plants and the pig, the dog, the rat. They burned the lands along the seacoasts for their agriculture. They hunted and exterminated many birds including the flightless giant birds, which some Hawaiian legends describe as big as a man! Before Captain Cook arrived, more than 35 endemic Hawaiian land birds had already become extinct.

But when western man hit these shores, the real destruction of this Garden of Eden began and in earnest. Not intentionally, of course. Cattle, goats, cats, mongooses, and pigs and rats more than twice the size of the Polynesian predators were set free. So were diseases. So were 10,000 alien plants.

The delicate plants and animals of the Garden, who had evolved no protection because they needed none, were gobbled up, trampled upon, exterminated at a rate tragically unbelievable. This was long before the days of the science of ecology, and the development in humans of an ecological conscience. Over 1,000 plants and animals have disappeared from the Garden since human colonization, and currently Hawaii has 317 threatened and endangered plant and animal species. The bell is tolling for Hawaiian nature. One-third of the US roster of endangered species is Hawaiian species. One-half, 50%, of native insects have disappeared forever.

Today, Hawaii is in the death throes of a full-scale alien invasion. Millions of tourists and the cargo-holds of ships and jetliners offer an easy road to paradise for hitchhiking alien plants, animals, and insects. Bird-eating snakes hide invidiously in the wheel wells of airplanes arriving from Guam. Visitors intentionally sneak in alien animals and plants as well; they unintentionally bring diseases. Seeds from exotic ornamental plants imported by well-meaning home gardeners escape from backyards to sprout and proliferate in dry forestland already more than decimated by human habitation.

There are about 150 distinctive ecosystems in the Hawaiian Islands. These ecosystems are so distinct that the Hawaiian Islands constitute a unique global bioregion. These ecosystems include tropical dry forests, subalpine grasslands, snowy alpine deserts, brackish anchialine pools, subterranean lava tube systems with eyeless creatures, and windswept coastal dunes. You name it; the islands have it.

Some native ecosystems have been very hard hit. Over 90% of Hawaiian lowland dry forests have been lost to agriculture, development, fire, or weed invasions. Other ecosystems have been relatively less impacted. Alpine deserts on the summit of Mauna Loa, for example, are very much as they were before humans came. Half of the 150 ecosystem types are in danger, imperiled by human-related alterations in the ecosystem. Most of the loss has occurred along the coasts and in the lowlands, where the majority of human habitation exists today, but the rainforests are greatly imperiled.

Hawaii is the Extinction Capital of the World. Over 75% of the United States extinctions have occurred here. We are also known as "The Endangered Species Capital of the World" with over 25% of the United States endangered species located

21

in Hawaii. Yet, Hawaii which has only 0.2% of the land area in the country!

Many more pests that are injurious now threaten to invade Hawaii and wreak further damage. The brown tree snake alone could forever change the character of our islands. Hawaii's future well being depends upon stopping and containing the influx of new pests. It is estimated that new species are being introduced to Hawaii at a rate that is 2 million times more rapid than the natural rate.

An amazing array of endemic plants and animals, which occur nowhere else on Earth, call the rainforest home. Soaring over forests of koa and 'ohia, endangered Hawaiian hawks search for prey among exotic vines where spectacular native tree snails hide. Forest birds such as the Hawaiian crow and Hawaiian thrush have no other habitat in which to live, except, tragically, cages. Ditto for native honeycreepers, birds that have evolved diverse bill structures for feeding on different plants in mesic and wet forests. Several marvelous carnivorous caterpillars are endemic to Hawaii. These fantastic creatures mimic twigs and snatch prey that mistakenly comes too close; others perch on tree trunks, or wait on ferns and leaves. When triggered by touch, these caterpillars snatch their unsuspecting prey.

Saving these unique and precious remaining native species and habitats is now a race against time.

Do you know, the tropical rainforests are the single greatest terrestrial source of air that we breathe? Often described as the Earth's lungs, the tropical rainforests take in vast quantities of carbon dioxide, a poisonous gas that mammals exhale, and through the process of photosynthesis, convert it into clean, breathable air.

Do you know that while the tropical rainforests cover just 2% of the Earth's land surface, they are home to two-thirds of all the living species on the planet?

Do you know that nearly half the medicinal compounds we use every day come from plants endemic to the tropical rainforest? Within some of the rainforest lava caves of Hawaii, for example, there exist bacteria that may be possible cures for cancer.

For all our calculations, no one can predict what will happen to Island biodiversity in the future, but perhaps clues can be found in the fiery nature of Hawaii itself. Every day, as fresh lava flows into the ocean, new land is formed—land that will, in time, become new habitat for Hawaiian plants and animals, both native and invasive. Life is change. Just as the geography of Hawaii is always changing, so will the shape of life on these wonderful Islands.

One thing is certain. Visitors to Hawaii are very blessed to experience this treasure as it is now.

Flora and Fauna

Native species of plants and animals are of two groups, endemic and indigenous. Endemic species are only found in Hawaii; they evolved here and are now distinct species from plants and animals elsewhere in the world. Indigenous species are found here and elsewhere; they may have evolved here or elsewhere. Both indigenous and endemic species arrived without human help.

Hawaii Volcanoes National Park has among the highest number, 54, of threatened and endangered plants and animals in the National Park System, mostly due to non-native species. The National Park Service is working aggressively to eradicate them.

Kilauea rainforest is unlike the other rainforests in the world in that, instead of many tree species, only one or two dominate the forest. The dominate canopy tree here is the beautiful red-blossomed 'ohi'a lehua, the subject of many myths and legends of Hawaii. The second canopy layer is composed of 'olapa. Understory trees are kawa'u, kolea, pilo, olomea, mamaki, and opuhe. Tree ferns, called hapu'u, the largest ferns in the world, are characteristic of Hawaii Island rainforests; they occur much less frequently, if at all, on the older islands.

The bio-diversity of Kilauea rainforest occurs in its understory and ground cover. Ferns are paramount, with many, many species, ranging from delicate and lacy, some even only one cell thick, to stout-trunked and stiff-textured. There are native peperomias, endemic hydrangeas, giant African violet relatives, as well as succulents of the lobelia family. There are few vines.

One feature of Hawaii rainforests is the epiphytes, plants that grow on tree trunks and branches of host plants. These epiphytes don't feed off their host plants; they live in harmony. A great example of a host pant is the hapu'u. You will often see myriad numbers of other plants growing on their trunks; these hapu'u are called "nurse logs." There is

24

also an abundance of mosses and liverworts in these rainforests.

Birds that you are likely to see and hear include the 'oma'o, which has among its calls a "police whistle," and the apapane, the beautiful brilliant red bird that flits among the same-colored lehua blossoms. Frequently you may also see the kalij pheasant, a non-native bird with a sweet, gurgling cry.

Other interesting animals include the predaceous caterpillar mentioned above, an inchworm "dragon" that captures prey by using sticks and leaf edges to perch upon and seize their unwary victims.

Dislike spiders? One arachnid might make you smile! It's the Happyface Spider, a translucent, yellow-bodied guy with red and black markings, who wears a smiley face on his back. These creatures live underneath leaves of plants. Interestingly, some of the spiders here may form new species with the time of a human lifespan, they evolve so quickly.

Entire biosystems may have their own speciated plants and animals. A single cave or pit crater may have a completely different biosystem from any other on the Island. A species of spider in one lava cave may be unable to reproduce with its cousin in a lava tube just a half-mile away.

One creature to avoid is the wild pig. These guys can get rough if cornered. Especially a sow with piglets should be avoided. Pigs can run fast!

That strange creature that looks like a little locomotive darting across the road or through the forest is a mongoose. Brought here to control rats, it has wiped out entire bird populations. Unfortunately, as it turned out, rats are nocturnal and mongooses (plural of mongoose!) are diurnal. They rarely meet. Unfortunately.

Culture

According to Hawaiian myths, Kilauea's violent eruptions are caused by Pele, the beautiful, hotheaded Goddess of Fire, during her frequent fits of temper. Pele historically was both revered and feared; her immense power and many adventures figure prominently in ancient Hawaiian songs and chants. Stamping her feet, she causes earthquakes. By digging with the pa'oe, her magic stick, she causes volcanic eruptions and fiery devastation.

Legend describes the long and bitter quarrel between Pele and her older sister Namakaokahai that led to the creation of the chain of volcanoes that form the Islands. Pele was seeking fire, and dug pits in succession on the islands of Kauai, Oahu, Molokai, and Maui as her sister pursued her from their homeland island far to the south. At Maui, however, Namakaokahai finally caught up with her, killed her, and scattered her bones in the sea.

Pele returned, however, as an eruptive cloud over the still-active volcanoes on the Big Island of Hawaii. Here she dug a pit, the volcanic caldera known as Kilauea, and at last made her home in smoking Halema'uma'u Crater. As always, she's given to anger, and vents her rage by spitting out rivers of hot lava to swallow up those who displease her. To placate her ire, islanders toss sacrifices into the crater, including bottles of rum! More than once, an advancing flow of lava has stopped just short of a vulnerable village soon after such a sacrifice.

Go figure!

Stories about Pele are endless. Local Hawaiians as well as haoles, as "newcomers" to the Islands are called, give her credence and respect. You will probably see offerings of ti leaves and flower leis left throughout the Park for the Madam. Besides appearing as a beautiful, tempestuous redhead, she is said sometimes to go about disguised as an old crone, sometimes with a little white dog. In this guise, she tests mortals' kindness to her.

I myself have a friend, whom I consider responsible and truthful, who said that one rainy night, out of pity, she stopped her car to offer one such old woman a ride. The woman told her she was Pele. She did not have her white dog with her.

According to King Kalakaua, there was an actual Pele clan. Driven from Samoa in the eleventh century, they made their home at Kilauea. Attacked by a hostile chief who desired to take one beautiful young Pele maiden for his lover, the Pele clan holed up in a cave, which, unfortunately, was inundated by fire and lava when the volcano erupted. Thus began the many myths of Pele.

By the way, there are still people on the Island with the last name "Pele."

How is it that Pele's home—black, smoky, and virtually barren—is cloaked in the rich greenery of the voluptuous rainforest? That's another well-known story, though there are many versions of it.

It seems that one of those smitten with her beauty was Kamapua'a, the pig demigod who could take many forms, one of which is the amau fern, one of the most prominent tree ferns of Kilauea, a fern covered with black, stiff bristles resembling those of a boar.

Kamapua'a got it into his head to woo the Madam by planting the lush green vegetation around her home while she was sleeping, much as these days a would-be suitor might leave a dozen red roses on his sweetheart's doorstep. Much to his chagrin, when Pele awoke and climbed out of her pit, she was enraged by what she saw.

She chased Kamapua'a and came close to catching him, so close that she burned his behind. The story tells us that the brilliant red amau fern frond, a form of the demigod, standing out in the sea of lush green, is a sign of the battle between Pele and Kamapua'a. These vibrant red fronds are called Ehupua'a, meaning "burnt-singed pig."

And that is how Halema'uma'u got its name, "house of the amau fern."

Another important goddess of Kilauea is Laka. She is the niece of Pele, and the goddess of the forest, the patron goddess of the hula, and sometimes she is considered the goddess of love. Also the Hawaiian goddess of plenty, the song, and the rainstorm, she is very popular and her cult includes the placing of wreaths on her sacred hula alter. If you allow yourself, you may get a fleeting glimpse of Laka in the dancing, gently swaying trees and plants of the rainforest.

Ancient Hawaiians did not live up here on Kilauea; it was too sacred and too scary! Pele might erupt at any time. Only solitary bird catchers and herb gatherers wandered the forest trails, though occasionally groups of warriors might cross the land. One such unlucky group had their footprints immortalized in the 1790 event of Keonehelelei, "the falling sands." You'll learn more about this fascinating occurrence when you read about "Footprints" later in this guide. It's a place I hope you can visit, one of my faves!

Caution!

Though Hawaii Volcanoes National Park and the Kilauea area may seem like Disneyland, it is not. You can get lost, and never be found. Just last year, one of our Village residents strolled into the forest for what she thought was to be a short walk—she was lost for two days.

Never allow small children to hike alone, or run on ahead of you—they might run over a cliff! Few places within the Park have guardrails of any kind. For the most part, especially if you are not an experienced hiker, do not go off trail—there are deep holes and lava tubes, usually hidden by brush, everywhere. Do not climb down into steam vents, as one young woman did a few years ago, and was cooked. And I already mentioned my friend who fell into a lava sea. Don't take chances just to get a good photo.

There is an old Hawaiian adage about walking on lava. Keep your mouth closed and your eyes to the ground. Good advice—, which I follow.

Be aware of what we call vog. Vog is a form of air pollution that results when sulfur dioxide and other gases and particles are emitted by the Volcano. It can cause headaches, watery eyes, sore throat, and breathing difficulties. These effects are especially pronounced in people with respiratory conditions and children. Most of the time, our wonderful trade winds blow the vog over to Kona, and we here in Volcano have great air, but once in a while the wind shifts, and we get vog. There will be a sign posted at the entrance to the Park proclaiming "poor air quality" if we have a bad day. Rare, but take notice. You may have to drive around with your windows up, or even leave the area.

Always hike with lots of water, and keep extra water bottles in the car.

Don't try to climb cliffs. They crumble! And of course, if lava is actively flowing, don't get too close—not only your shoes but you will melt!

If you hike alone, be extremely cautious. Let someone know where you are going and when you plan to return. Take a GPS device if possible, or a compass. Especially observe these rules if you hike alone in the Footprints area or The Place of the Guardians.

With that said, enjoy yourselves to the max! We have no snakes!

Ready for the adventure of a lifetime?…
Let's go!

The entrance fee into the Park is $10 per car, and is good for one week. As you drive through the Park entrance, ask for a free map! With the map, and my instructions, you can visit Kilauea's most fascinating sights.

This guide is divided into sites along Crater Rim Drive, sites along Chain of Craters Road, and sites outside of the gated entrance, including Volcano Village.

Crater Rim Drive formerly was a 13-mile loop around Kilauea Caldera. Since Halema'uma'u began emitting her toxic plume three years ago, almost the entire southern portion of the loop as been closed. Therefore, this guide through the gated area of the Park will take you in two opposite directions on Crater Rim Drive, beginning from the Visitor Center.

We'll start first heading west from the Visitor Center, counterclockwise, after a stop at the Park Center.

Hawaii Volcanoes National Park
Visitor Center

Getting there: from Hilo, it's 30 miles south on Highway 11 (a 45 minute drive); from Kailua-Kona, it's a 96 mile drive southeast on Highway 11 (2 to 2 1/2 hour drive). You can't miss it.

Make the Visitor Center your first stop. Here you can get maps, updates on volcanic activity, browse the bookstore, and watch fantastic movies of eruptions. Pick up the free maps to use as an adjunct to this guide.

I highly recommend the exciting movie of the 1959 Kilauea I'ki eruption, which is usually shown only once a day. It's fabulous, and in color. You get a real feel for Kilauea Volcano from it. Call ahead to ask what time it is shown: 985-6000. It's free, of course.

There are wonderful and informative displays of Kilauea flora and fauna, featuring the recorded sounds of our rare birds. You can also talk story with the very friendly Park rangers. There are free guided hikes and lectures: times and places are posted by nine-thirty each morning on the board just outside the center. These are all worthwhile.

You can also obtain camping permits (free) from the rangers; though not many rangers are out in the backcountry, it is wise to let them know where you are, just in the case of an eruption. It has happened that they have had to evacuate campers and hikers in life-threatening situations, such as unannounced lava flows.

Be sure to fill your water bottles with Kilauea's delicious, filtered rainwater; the tap is just outside the center by the restrooms.

The historic Volcano House with its rooms, restaurants and shops is now open again after years-long renovations. You can stay here, eat at the restaurant with the commanding view of Halema'uma'u, and gets snacks. A great thing to do in the evening is get a glass of wine at the bar and then sit in one of the big comfy chairs in front of the glass windows and watch the sun go down and the glow over the Volcano begin. A cheap and great date!

If you are military personnel or retired military, you may shop at the little store in the Kilauea Military Camp just a few miles from the Visitor Center, on the way to Jaggar Museum. They do ask for military documentation. However, anyone can get refreshments in their cafeteria. There's a post office and bowling alley as well. If it's after five, you may get gas there too, at the self-serve pumps, even if you are not military. On Friday afternoons, there is a great discount at the gas pump.

Volcano Art Gallery

If you're art-inclined, the Volcano Art Gallery is just a few steps west from the Visitor's Center. This was the original 1877 Volcano House, and you can have fun reading the roster of comments in the guest books by visitors, including notables such as Mark Twain.

The Gallery features several hundred great artists whose work is inspired by Kilauea, and you will find some of the best art in Hawaii here, as the Volcano Art Gallery is very selective. Have a look at the wonderful pit-fired "aumakua" (divine guardian) "artifacts" which are usually displayed right on top of the jewelry cases. These are unique, small and make great gifts. If you are looking for woodwork, especially koa, this is the place! If you hit it just right, you might want to attend one of the opening shows. You can ask the great people at the Gallery when the next event is.

The Gallery also sponsors workshops, classes, special lectures and hula performances. Their website is www.volcanoartcenter.org. The Gallery is open every day from nine to five, except Christmas.

Sulfur Banks

You can walk to the Sulfur Banks by taking the trail just a few minutes from the Visitor's Center and Volcano Art Gallery, or, you can drive a half-mile and park at the Steam Vents and walk back a short distance, cross the road and access the walking trail. It's simple to find. From Visitor's Center, turn west, the opposite direction from the Park entrance. Take the sidewalk trail past the Art Center. Follow it until it forks, and take the right fork as it descends downward.

Do you know what sulfur smells like? Rotten eggs! This area is filled with fumaroles, which are holes in volcanic areas from which hot smoke and gases escape. If you have heart or respiratory problems, or if you are pregnant or have children, you should avoid this area.

This fascinating place, which might remind you of Yellowstone, was anciently called Ha'akulamanu, which means "like a birds' gathering place." It was famous for both its birds and its healing vapors. The gases inhibited the growth of deep-rooted trees, creating habitat for foraging birds, including nene, the state bird, and other geese and ducks.

The lovely boarded walk is bounded by 'ohia lehua trees, bamboo orchids, and many types of ferns, including the abundant false stag horn fern. There are several benches where you can rest, have a snack, take pics and enjoy the views.

There is a lovely view of Mauna Loa at the top of the boardwalk, if it isn't clouded over. I like to come here in the afternoon, when it is usually sunny, bask in the sunshine while sitting on the bench, and absorb the majesty of the biggest mountain on Earth. At this time of day, Mauna Loa takes on lovely subdued hues of deep purples, blues and grays, which contrast beautifully with the golds, silvers, pinks, and ivory shades of the sedge grasses. Wintertime is especially beautiful here; the low lighting of the sun makes this a stunning place to photograph.

Surface water leaking into cracks, where it is heated to high temperatures, rises as steam and toxic gasses here, turning the earth a reddish color, and coating the rocks with beautiful crystals, such as the yellow sulfur crystals. Please don't hop off the boardwalk to gather crystals; not only is it unlawful and disrespectful, but you can be severely burned if your foot goes through the sometimes shallow earth. It has happened! Keep your children on the trail, for their safety.

You can retrace your steps, or cross the road and walk over to Steam Vents.

**Steaming Bluff
(Steam Vents)**

Steam Vents is a five-minute drive from the Park Center, or you can take the trail past the Art Center, as just described above. Although steam vents occur throughout the Park, this is a great place to and stop see them up close. These are fumaroles of steam but no gasses, so you can get very near and even feel the heat. Just to one side, clearly marked, is access to the Crater Rim Trail, which runs approximately 13 miles around the entire Kilauea Caldera, though portions are now closed due to the toxic cloud spouting at Halema'uma'u. If you want to, from here you can walk all the way (about a mile) to the Jaggar Museum Volcano Observatory and back, rather than drive. I recommend it. It's lovely especially on a full moon evening. Or, perhaps you might just want to stroll the trail a short distance and peer over the cliff. Don't get too close to the edge! It crumbles easily and there might be an overhang.

The Steam Vents steam more just after a heavy rain; that's because the water seeps down, down, down to the hot cracks, is heated, and rises up again as vapor. These vents, unlike the one ones across the street at Sulfur Banks, are not toxic but they are hot!

Kilauea Overlook
and
Uwekahuna Bluff

Continuing .7 miles along Crater Rim Drive by car, or hiking Crater Rim Trail toward the south, as just described above, you reach Kilauea Overlook, one of the best views of the caldera, and much less crowded than the view at Jaggar Museum. Colorful, sacred offerings of stones wrapped in ti leaves and leis of flowers are often left here on the ground or hung about in trees. The steep bluff overlooking the caldera is Uwekahuna Bluff, which means "Wailing Priest." This is where ancient and modern priests made and make their offerings. Be careful, as I said above, not to step too close to the edge; many places along the cliff are undercut and the rock is fragile and easily shatters—it's a long way down!

There are covered picnic tables here just to the side of the trail, but at lunchtime, these are usually taken by the bicycle tourists. Plan lunch earlier than eleven or later than one o'clock if you want to use the tables. Otherwise, if it is not wet, spread a blanket on the ground and enjoy!

Kilauea Overlook is especially beautiful at night and at dawn. If you can, plan to come in the dark. And better yet, come on a full moon. This is a great place to meditate on eternity, on birth, on death. What better place to contemplate such things than at the edge of the most active volcano on Earth?

This is perhaps the best overlook of Halema'uma'u, the House of Everlasting Fire, the home of the fire goddess herself, who is also the goddess of death and rebirth. One of her names is Ka Wahine 'ai Honua, the woman who devours the land. She's often depicted as a wanderer, and people claim to have sighted her all over the Islands, but especially around here, in Kilauea. If you meet a beautiful woman here, or an old beggar woman with a white dog asking for food or drink, be nice to her! Those who are unkind to her are punished by having their lands consumed by lava.

I often sit on the big rocks near the edge of the cliff overhang (but not *too* close), kept silent company by only a few skeletal, grey 'ohia trees that stand like strange, many-armed sentinels in the moonshine. On a cold and clear night (and if it is clear here at the Volcano, it will be cold—bring a good jacket!), the stars of the Milky Way spread out across the inky-blue sky like a celestial mantle, and the moon hangs high in the sky like a gleaming skull. The three-mile-wide crater looks like a moonscape; huge black boulders are strewn across the otherwise barren and silvery landscape, casting bloated, malformed shadows across the caldera floor. Transparent, whitish steam rises like mute, wispy specters from scattered vents on the floor of the crater, curling and trailing and disappearing into thin air, and the congealed iridescent black lava lake contrasts eerily with the white-striated walls of the caldera. Awed into complete silence by the otherworldly spectacle before me, sometimes the hair on my arms stands up.

Three hundred feet below, the pit crater, Halema'uma'u, the House of Everlasting Fire, the home of Goddess Pele, glows an intense fiery red-orange. Like a huge, silent ghost, a thick white plume rolls from out of the pit, billowing into the sky high above the caldera, spiraling off toward the sea and the stars, unceasingly.

It is said that once here on or near this cliff, a house stood over a pit; if anyone entered, the priest pulled ropes which made the floor collapse and cause the person to fall to his death. Later, a hero by the name of Kamiki torched the house and the priest wept. That is why the bluff here is called Uwekahuna. "Uwe" means to wail, and "kahuna" means priest.

Sometimes, sitting out here alone on cold, clear full moon nights, I have almost heard the priest keening in the wind.

Aia la o Pele. There is Pele.

The glow in the plume is caused by the rising and falling lava lake in the crater within a crater within a crater below. There are maybe as many as seven pit craters, each inside the other. Just below the surface, a molten lava lake, pure magma, is sloshing and churning and boiling. The red glow you see is the reflection of the lake. That plume is made up of incredibly toxic gases. We could have a full-on eruption at any time.

Though the scene below, the moonlight and starlight illuminating the ghostly white plume issuing out of the red glow may be eerily soundless, you may sense a vibration just below the threshold of sound, a feeling just below the brink of hearing, coming up through the souls of your feet. It's the movement and flowing of the molten lava below. That's why we have the earthquakes almost everyday; the earth is moving and shifting. Most people aren't sensitive enough to feel it. But I feel it when I lie in bed at night.

Thomas Jaggar Museum
and

Hawaii Volcano Observatory

At the Jaggar Museum, located next door to the Hawaiian Volcano Observatory, which is closed to the public, you cannot only get an up-close view of Halema'uma'u but you can watch the seismographs, which are fascinating. The rangers give informative lectures usually twice daily and there is a bookstore here. Admission is free. The museum is open daily from 8:30 a.m. to 5 p.m.

You can learn all about volcanoes, and there are great displays of different types of lava ejecta—my faves are the ones called Pele's tears and Pele's hair. Pele's hair is made of volcanic glass threads formed when particles of molten material are thrown into the air and spun out by the wind into long hair-like strands. The diameter of the strands is less than 0.5 mm, and they can be as long as 2 meters and are a deep yellow or gold. Pele's tears are small pieces of solidified lava drops formed when airborne particles of molten material fuse into tear like drops of volcanic glass. They are jet black in color and are often found on one end of a strand of Pele's hair.

That great hole below you was a molten lake until 1924. During Captain Cooks' time, Halema'uma'u Crater was 800 ft deep and a lava lake was formed. It was only 1500 feet across. In 1924, Halema'uma'u Crater erupted explosively. Hot magma at a temperature of 2100 degrees Fahrenheit reached the base of the crater. Throughout the eruption, hot molten lava filled up the crater and formed a lava lake. The lava lake then drained to the east of Kilauea. Huge blocks of the crater wall were melted and torn off by the lava flows. The drainage of the lava lake caused the base of the crater to thin and groundwater broke through the crust, reaching the hot lava and causing a series of huge steam explosions. Water and lava doesn't mix too well!

The eruption in 1924 caused Halema'uma'u to increase in size to 3000 ft wide and 1200 ft deep. Numerous eruptive episodes since then have filled the crater to its present form. The last major eruption occurred in 1967. Lava from the 1967 eruption once filled up the crater to 100 ft below its rim. Lava then drained back into the magma chamber. Halema'uma'u Crater is now mostly covered by lava from the 1974 eruption.

The view here is fab. Not only can you peer into the yawning mouth of smoking Halema'uma'u, but you can look for miles off into the Ka'u desert. Ask a ranger to point out Mauna Ulu if it is clear. Mauna Ulu is a place you probably will visit later.

You can be mesmerized a long time by the spiral path of the volcanic plume. The gases almost always blow to the southeast, which is why the road from this point on is closed. Formerly, the Crater Rim Drive offered world-class cycling; I often used to cycle around the thirteen mile scenic route in awe, but I won't anymore unless the Goddess stops venting.

You may see beautiful white birds soaring gracefully above the crater. These are koa'e, white tailed tropicbirds. They feed in the sea, but they nest here in the crater walls.

If you look toward the south, you can spot the Southwest Rift, a great series of cracks running from

Kilauea's summit all the way to the sea. That means you are standing upon a major earthquake fault!

****

Around Crater Rim
Clockwise

Retracing the route back to the Park Center, take your time, don't let tailgaters push you, and enjoy the changes of scenery. The next portion of this guide begins at the Park Center, traveling in a clockwise direction. So drive back toward the Park gate. From the Park Visitor Center, the second right will be Crater Rim Drive, which will take you to all the wonderful sights on Chain of Craters Road.

First stop—Kilauea I'ki, "Little Kilauea."

Kilauea I'ki Overlook
and
Kilauea I'ki Trail

Kilauea I'ki is not to be missed! Even if you just park and peer out into the crater, this is a scene you will always remember. Just 50 years ago, in 1959, the highest and hottest lava fountain ever recorded in Hawaiian history, 1900 feet! spewed spectacular fireworks like never seen before, creating a wide, flat lake of black lava 414 feet deep. Looking down 500 feet onto the congealed lava, which appears as a sea of black waves, people appear as ants traversing the caldera floor, still steaming through cracks and rifts in the crust. Notice the hill of red cinder cone. We will be walking past it.

If you can, hike this one! You can go either in a clock or clockwise direction. Most people hike counter-clockwise, but I prefer clockwise. I'll describe the clockwise route here. This a four mile loop—doable by most people in 2-3 hours. I often see little children happily trekking along, as well as babies on their mother or father's back. (I also often see tired little children happily being carried on someone's back.) Fairly elderly people also can do this hike, though, remember, there is a 400 feet climb back out of the caldera.

You must take water, and I recommend light rain gear. Weather conditions can change in a moment. Wearing layers is best, because it can be chilly or very hot, all in one hike! You might also take sunscreen.

The path begins in the high rain forest. At Kilauea I'ki overlook, facing the caldera, head up the path to your left. As you traverse the lush tropical jungle, you will meet the King (the koa tree) and Queen (the 'ohia lehua tree) of the forest and their minions, the native plants and animals of the islands, of which more than 90% are endemic, found nowhere else on planet Earth. There are several scenic viewpoints along the first part of the half-mile path; stop and take them in.

Notice the deep cracks on your left. These are the kinds of cracks you can fall into if you go off trail!

In a half-mile, the trail comes to the Thurston Lava Tube parking lot. Stay on the sidewalk on the same side of the road, and the trail picks up again in just a few yards.

Descending into the crater via a switchback trail, you will experience the surreal, thrilling one-mile walk across what once was a molten lava lake, now hardened ropey pahoehoe and sharp, treacherous a'a lava, surrounded by 500 foot cliffs. Where else in the world can you walk on lava in the caldera of a volcano active only 50 years ago? Hawks, kolea birds and clouds soar high overhead, as you pass Pu'u Pua'i (Gushing Hill) cinder cone.

Notice the stacks of rocks. These are *ahu*; originally the native Hawaiians used them to mark boundaries. Here a few mark the trail. But all these at the beginning of the trail are a sort of statement by some tourists—as in *Kilroy was here*! Some are quite precariously balanced. The Park discourages such artistic statements as being culturally inappropriate and occasionally the Rangers come around and knock them down.

You don't have to stay on the trail here, but do remember the Hawaiian adage regarding walking on lava—keep your mouth shut and your eyes to the ground. Take your time and stroll over to some of the steam vents. You might notice some pipes sticking out of the ground. These are drill holes used to measure the lava lake's temperature and rate of solidification. Also, it is of interest that the NASA moon rover was tested in this crater. Not hard to see why.

Pu'u Pua'i, the big red cinder cone about half way across the crater, is the mouth from which all the lava that filled the lake was belched. You can get very close for a good look. There is a little path up over the hillock that is safe to walk. Just be careful. This is a good place to scout around and look at the titanium lava rocks, the beautiful rainbow-hued shards that change colors in the sunlight. Don't take any, though. Strictly forbidden! Besides, they don't seem to sparkle once removed from their home.

As you head toward the far end of the caldera, look down at the ground. If it's a sunny day, you will see millions of green glinting crystals; these are olivine crystals. Again, admire but don't take any as souvenirs. If everyone took some, soon …

As you climb up the steep steps, and they are steep, take your time and stop frequently to get your breath and admire the view back into the caldera. If you look back at Pu'u Pua'i, you can see the scars where molten lava slipped down the cone.

The caldera may be hot and windy, cold and rainy, misty or foggy—whatever! And conditions may change in a moment! I've never seen snow (ha!) but once I was caught in a majestic though frightening lightening storm when I was the only person down there. (Duh!) Often, ethereal rainbows appear like magic through the steaming vents on the caldera floor. You can see them on misty days after crossing the first half of the crater. Just turn around and look back toward where you have traversed. I've had the thrill of walking into one.

Truly an alien landscape, Kilauea I'ki may make you feel as if you have been on the moon!

At the top of the steps, turn right. Here you will see a bench. A nice place to stop and get your breath. Then continue on, bearing right at the first intersection, which is marked. Soon you will start climbing up again. When you reach the jumble of big boulders, take a rest and admire the view of Halema'uma'u. These boulders are the result of landslides from earthquakes of 1975 and 1983. In a little bit more of a climb, the trail flattens out—the hard part is over! Now you can just wander leisurely the one-mile back to the Kilauea Iki parking lot and enjoy the lush rainforest.

Thurston Lava Tube (Nahuku)

Less then a half-mile from the Kilauea I'ki overlook, you will come to the parking lot for Thurston Lava Tube. You might want to bring a flashlight, thought the cave is lit.

Nahuku (the Protuberances), known more commonly as Thurston Lava Tube, is one of the most visited sites in the park. Everyone is fascinated by caves!

Tip! Come in the morning, before nine, or in the evening, after five. Otherwise, due to its popularity, you may not find a parking place. Nahuku Lava Tube, known also as Thurston Lava tube, is one of the few lava tubes that are open to the public.

Nahuku Crater is an emerald jewel set within the Hawaiian rainforest, with its delicate lacy ferns hanging like lace curtains over the mouth of prehistoric and VERY eerie Thurston lava tube.

The trail consists of a short walk down into the crater through dense vegetation as it descends. The trail then goes through a short section of the 600 feet lava tube. This portion is well lit and has a macadam floor; that is why there are puddles of rainwater that have seeped down through the ceiling of the cave. Those long, stringy things hanging from the ceiling are roots of 'ohia trees. It's awesome to reflect that just a few hundred years ago, a river of molten red lava rushed through this lava tube thirty miles to the sea.

Emerging through a natural skylight, the trail loops back to some (be prepared—primitive) bathrooms and then the starting point.

You used to have the option of continuing through the cave but this option is no longer available, unfortunately, because this is the most interesting section of the lava tube. In the past, you could climb down into this part of the tube very warily, and if you dared, make your way very, very carefully all the way to the end. You would have to skirt huge boulders and fallen piles of rocks and hop over puddles of rainwater. You could marvel at the frozen black lava "push-ups" on the floor of the cave (remember those ice-cream push-ups? These lava push-ups are named for those!) and the sparkling rainbow titanium "drinking straws" that dangle from the lofty cathedral-like ceiling.

At the end of the cave, you could turn off your flashlights, sit in total darkness, and total silence, on a newly-fallen-from-the-ceiling lava stone "bench," (happened in the summer of 2010! Yikes!) and listen to the haunting sound of water drops seeping through the roof of the cave.

But not any more! That convenient newly- fallen stone bench is now covered with a many-ton portion of the ceiling of the cave! Luckily, it fell at night when no one happened to be sitting there! For now, for safety's sake, this portion of the tube is closed.

If you are really adventurous, you can visit the open part of Nahuku at night. It's permitted by Park regulations. My friends and I sometimes come here, go deep into the cave, and chant the Hallelujah chorus. Awesome!

Devastation Trail and Desolation Peak

Desolation Peak can be accessed from two directions. You can go by way of hiking across Byron's Ledge, from the direction of Kilauea I'ki, or you can drive to it.

Consult the free Park map for the Byron's Ledge route. There are several trails depending on where you hiking from. I like to come out of Kilauea I'ki Crater and continue on, taking the first path to the left at the top of the steps. If you go toward the bench, you are going in the wrong direction. After about an eight-mile of trail, turn left at a path junction, and almost immediately you will see a gate. Go through the gate (keep it closed because of pigs), and then through a lovely forest path carpeted with gold moss, called by locals the Yellow-brick Road.

If you hike this way, there are several views of Kilauea Caldera that are wonderful. You can stop on

Byron's Ledge for great photographs at several places; just follow the not so easy to discern short paths to the right that go to the edge, but *do be careful.* There is a real cliffhanger among giant ferns for another spectacular view and photographs of Halema'uma'u, just a few footsteps after going through the gate. *Be cautious!*

Keep to the left when you come to the sign which says a portion of the path is closed.

The terrain changes as you approach the climb up to Desolation Peak, becoming remarkably drier and warmer, until the path itself becomes pure cinder. Pu'u Pua'i, the red cinder cone of Kilauea Iki, comes again into sight on your left, but from this vantage point, appears as a perfect curve of blondish-reddish earth, Pele's Breast. Above is the ghostly Desolation Peak, and all around are the bleached white bones of trees and cinder pit craters, just as they were left by Kilauea I'ki's eruption of 1959. As you climb the crunchy hill, through 'ohi'a trees sometimes loaded with crimson red lehua blossoms, superb views of Mauna Loa and Mauna Kea arise before your eyes; that is, weather permitting, for sometimes the mountains are blanketed by eerie fog and mist.

To return, retrace your steps to the gate. Instead of turning right after the gate, continue straight ahead until you come to the next junction, about an eighth-mile. You will see a bench. Turn right, keep going, and you will access the trail back to Kilauea Iki parking lot. Just climb up, and continue straight ahead.

The easy way, of course, to reach Devastation Trail is to drive past Thurston Lava Tube, continuing on about two miles (lots of curves, watch for cyclists) past the first road on the right (Pu'u Pua'i Overlook) to the next road on the right. Here you will find a large parking area.

There are two trails; the paved one-half mile trail leads to Pu'u Pua'i Overlook. Do take it; the trail itself is interesting and you can totter on the sheer cliff side and look down into Kilauea I'ki. There is also a picnic table here, one of the few in the Park, and it is usually available. A wonderful place to lunch.

The other unpaved trail is even more interesting. It's really just a short walk to Desolation Peak.

This area was a large 'ohi'a forest, but when Kilauea I'ki blew up in 1959, the trees were denuded; the white bleached bones of the trees still lay as they fell. Looks like a holocaust and so it was.

As you walk along, note the many ohelo bushes with their bright red berries. These are the berries sacred to Madam Pele. You can sample them (just a few; this area is the nene lunch area) but be sure to toss the first one to the Goddess, as is customary. Otherwise, you might invoke her ire. I'm not kidding!

Notice also the many small pit craters. I sometimes come here at night, climb down the side of one of the little indentions, spread a blanket out, and watch shooting stars. It's quite comfy; I can lean against the side of the crater, not have to crane my neck, and be out of the wind.

You'll know when you reach Desolation Peak. Just below it, the cinder road descends back down into the rain forest. This is one of the best places to photograph the entirety of Mauna Loa, that is, if it is not obscured by mist.

On a clear day, you will be able to see Halema'uma'u, Mauna Loa and also Mauna Kea, which will look just like a little bump on the horizon compared to Long Mountain. In wintertime, the mountains can be shrouded in a mantle of snow, which is especially majestic. You can also see as far as the Ka'u desert.

Because the weather is so changeable here, the view is always different. Late evening and nighttime viewing can be especially lovely, but do dress warmly. Most nights, the wind picks up and it is quite chilly, if not downright cold. If you're a photographer, you might get some lovely photographs as the light changes in the evening. Mauna Loa turns all silvery, and the stars are lovely.

Chain of Craters Road

The Chain of Craters Road is one of the most scenic drives in the world! Down, down, and more down you go, more than 4000 feet to the sea, and all along the way are volcanic wonders. An enormous lava flow in 1995 severed the road that once linked the Park with Kalapana. What goes down must come back up, so at the end of the road, you must turn around and drive back up. It's almost 40 miles round trip. Well worth it!

To reach Chain of Craters Road from the entrance to the park take a left onto Crater Rim Drive just after you pass the Park entrance gate. Follow

Crater Rim Drive for three miles, past Thurston lava tube, until you reach Devastation Trail. Turn left directly across from the Devastation Trail parking lot. Not hard to find at all.

Chain of Craters Road may be one of the most unique experiences you have on the Big Island, or on the planet! Stretching almost 19 miles and going from 4,000 ft. elevation to sea level, this scenic drive along the East Rift Zone of the volcano is pock-marked with craters of varying shapes and sizes, as well as lava flows, petroglyphs, and, possibly, active lava. Along this road are many interesting hikes, breathtaking vistas, and the opportunity to see the handiwork of Madam Pele.

There are no special facilities or services along the way, other than simple toilets (well named "pit-stops"). These are located at Mauna Ulu, mile marker 3.6, and at the very end of the road. Come prepared with plenty of drinking water and sunscreen. A hat and good walking shoes are recommended.

The road begins in the lush forest, but as you descend, enormous vistas of geologic wonders unroll before your eyes. Many craters, each with their distinctive characteristics, dot the landscape. You may want to stop at a lot of them.

Place of the Guardians
(Pele's Playground)

Where is this wonderful place?

Just northwest of Lua Manu Crater, the first crater along Chain of Craters Road. There are two ways to get there.

In both cases, please take plenty of water.

The easiest and safest access is the portion of Crater Rim Trail just above Lua Manu. The path is clearly marked "Crater Rim Trail," and it cuts across the highway, about an eighth mile after a left on Chain of Craters Road. Place of the Guardians is on the same side of the road as Lua Manu, that is, on your right as you go down Chain of Craters. There is a parking place just across the road.

However, because of the toxic plume coming from Halema'uma'u, at present there may be a sign stating that this portion of the Crater Rim Trail is closed. Up to you, if you know what I mean. If you do take the trail, you follow it approximately one-half mile through grassy, scrubby forestland. When you come to the place where you see the congealed lava flow on your left, walk in. In just a few yards, you will be on the flow. There is no path, so you are on your own. Be careful.

The other legal way to enter is just to park at Lua Manu and hike behind it. Again, take care; **there is no path**. You are walking on what is called shelly lava; it is like walking on seashells, extremely fragile.

This is a place that few people know about. It's really special! However, if you go here, please be very cautious. This is terrain where you can easily sprain an ankle, break a leg, take a very bad fall or get cut badly or worse on the very sharp a'a lava. Basically, this is like walking on glass or razor blades. You need to wear really good footwear, preferably jeans, a hat and take water. Don't go alone!

With these warnings, let me describe this incredible place.

Know what a projective test is? It's a personality test designed to let a person respond to ambiguous stimuli, presumably revealing hidden emotions and internal conflicts. An example of such a test is the Rorschach the inkblot test. Well, this fantastic landscape is like a projective test.

Do you see The Igneous, a strange race of creatures made of living rock and magma, and alien to the eyes of humanity? Do you see Magmaarghs, huge, hideous creatures made of lava who look incredibly deranged, with strange eyes and huge mouths? Do you see Magmion and his hordes of creatures made from charred earth out to destroy and consume the souls of Gore?

Or do you see whimsical, quirky and comical composite beasts such as giant owls, half dolphin-half dog creatures, and perhaps a colossal cookie monster?

Perhaps you see all of the above as you take in this gallery of the imagination, where monsters and other whimsical, fantastic creatures play in a totally surreal landscape? Maybe this strange fantasyland with its inspired creatures bears the echoes of childhood dreams and nightmares?

Whatever! You have to admit, Pele had a great time playing here! A real flight of fancy!

This eerie landscape, created by the July 1974 lava flow, is the very best of lava trees and lava tree molds in the Islands, and virtually unknown. You won't find it on Park maps, and I have never found a reference to it in any of the guidebooks.

How did it happen?

Lava moved through a forest of 'ohi'a trees and submerged the lower 3-5 meters of the moist trunks. As the peak flow passed through the area, the surface of the flow subsided, leaving the trunks of trees standing above the new ground surface coated with a skin of solidified lava.

What was left are casts of trees that were in the way of a lava flow. One would think that the trees would have been demolished by the flow, but these lava trees are proof this does not always happen. Lava trees form when lava flows over a forested area and the lava begins to cool around the trees and later burns through to the inside of the trunk. This leaves a hollow mold in the middle of the lava tree, though sometimes part of the charred tree is left over. The inside of the trees show the original texture of the bark. The lava that flowed through the area here must have deflated because the trees are positive features on the landscape instead of holes in the ground.

We know this was a short-lived eruption. The height of the tree molds shows the highest level of lava flow. The direction of flow can be determined using tree molds by observing the seam that forms when lava wraps around the tree—the seam is opposite to the direction of flow. Lava trees are formed only by thin flows, but tree molds are preserved in both thin and thick flows. Both structures may indicate the direction of flow of the lava in which they are preserved.

Some of the best formations are toward the back, deeper across the flow. My very favorite is "The Embrace," sometimes called "Tantric Couple."

I myself do not come here often; one reason is that I feel it is too dangerous to hike alone. But I do love the ambiance; I come here in times of personal crisis when I feel I need the special assistance of…The Guardians.

Continuing on Chain of Craters Road...

Pit craters such as Lua Manu (Bird Pit), the first crater on the right side of the road as you descend, and many others along the Chain of Craters Road, formed primarily when lava drained out of chambers beneath the surface, causing the surface to collapse inward to fill the void. These craters are characterized by deep pits with no debris on the rims, indicating a lack of eruptive events in their formation.

Most of the pit craters along Chain of Craters Road were formed before written records were kept, but their formation is likely associated with the major subsidence episodes around 1790 that formed much of the modern Kilauea Crater seen today.

Notice the number of bees flying over Lua Manu. Since "manu" means "flying," this could just as well be called "bee pit."

Puhimau Crater (Ever Smoking), approximately one mile down the road, is a pit crater that formed between about 1450 and 1800. You might try singing into this crater; sometimes, you can hear your echo.

Between Puhimau and the next crater, there are acres of dead and dying vegetation on the right side of the road, the Thermal Hotspot. In 1938, this area was about 15 acres large; by 1985, it had increased to 29 acres. Today trees are dying on this side of the road, suggesting an increase in size since 1985. A geochemical study done in 1977 showed higher than usual concentrations of volatile materials, including helium, mercury, carbon dioxide, and various sulfur compounds rising from the ground in the thermal area, suggesting the presence of magma below. It is suspected that the Puhimau Thermal Area, as this area is called, is in the early stages of pit crater formation. That means things are happening here!

Ko'oko'olau Crater (named for a medicinal plant) is 1.5 miles down the road. Ko'oko'olau Crater is an excellent example of what happens to a crater after about 200 years of an absence of lava. The crater is completely overgrown with native forest.

At approximately mile marker 2.2, look for a small unmarked pullout on the right. Park and walk across the road to a dirt path. The path leads about 50 feet to the edge of a sheer cliff, which drops off into the abyss. This massive 150 ft. wide by 165 ft. deep crater is called Devil's Throat, appropriately named! You are on your own, so take care—there are no guardrails to block you so very carefully step around the crumbling edges of the pit. It was formed in early 1912. It's very deep with vertical walls. It's rumored that this is where law enforcement dispose of confiscated pot plants.

Park rangers discourage tourists from visiting this crater; a "Danger No Entry" sign is posted just before the crater rim.

Hilina Pali Road

At 2.2 miles down Chain of Craters, on the right, is the Hilina Pali Road. Few tourists go here. This narrow and rough nine-mile paved road ends at Hilina Pali Lookout.

The Hilina Pali Road starts through scrub with scattered trees. After a stretch of pahoehoe lava, vegetation varies greatly, from open scrub forest to desert. You will pass the Mauna Iki trailhead, and the Kulanaokuaiki Campground, and then come to a former campground, now closed for nene protection, Kipuka Nene. This is an area of open and closed forest of 'ohi'a trees, spared by recent lava flows. Beyond is another area of pahoehoe lava desert, then another forested kipuka, then lava desert again. After this, on rather older lava, is a savanna. You will pass another kipuka and then the road ends at Hilina Pali, a great fault scarp 450 m high. This is part of the semi-arid Ka'u desert.

Kulanaokuaiki Campground is located at 2,700-foot elevation and about 5 miles down the Hilina Pali Road. There is no water. There are three campsites; two of these sites are wheelchair accessible. There are barbecue grills, a toilet (no running water), and picnic tables.

The road ends on the rift. Two trails continue, one down the hill to the coast, and another into the desert, along the top of the cliff. There is a shelter with a water catchment system. There is a small cairn north of the shelter that marks an interesting freshwater crack where you can take a refreshing dip. The other trail is the Mauna Iki trail (9.6 level miles round trip). It leads through meadowlands to a cabin at Kipuka Pepeiao where there is also water. The downhill trail switchbacks steeply down to the coast to Ka'aha Point, about 8 miles roundtrip. Located 7.7 miles from the nearest trailhead, the Halape Campsite offers a small sandy beach where hikers can camp under the coconut trees.

Check with rangers at the Park Center for current information on this trail.

Continuing on Chain of Craters Road...

Hi'iaka Crater (the Sisters of Pele) is a small collapse pit, formed in 1968 and further modified in 1973 by lava that flowed from both nearby vents. Hi'iaka Crater is located approx. 2.4 miles along Chain of Craters Road.

Pauahi Crater (the Fire is Out!) is located 3.2 miles along Chain of Craters Road. Pauahi Crater consists of three overlapping prehistoric pit craters. These craters cut across prehistoric lava flows and ash layers roughly 350-500 years old. Pauahi was active as recently as 1979.

Three eruptions have occurred near Pauahi Crater in historical time, in 1973 and 1979. The November 1973 eruption lasted a total of 31 days. Two fissures opened within minutes of each other, and lava began to pool in both the east and west pits of the crater. The lava flowed in from the fissures, also erupting from the crater itself, creating a huge lava lake at the bottom of the crater. The November 1979 eruption lasted only one day and was preceded by a number of small earthquakes. During the peak of the earthquake swarm, as many as 20 earthquakes per hour shook the ground beneath the Pauahi Crater area.

Coming up are two of my favorite places are Pu'u Huluhulu and Mauna Ulu. Take the road to the left, clearly marked, 3.5 miles down the road. This is also the place to access the Napau Crater Trailhead.

Pu'u Huluhulu

Pu'u Huluhulu (Shaggy Hill) is a cinder and spatter cone that was built by eruptions about 300 to 400 years ago. Pu'u Huluhulu is a kipuka, a place where lava has flowed all around but left a swath of island unscathed. At this kipuka, early in the morning, rare forest birds may be seen and heard. On a clear day, the view is unsurpassed in the islands— you can see Mauna Loa, Mauna Kea, Pu'u 'O'o and the Pacific Ocean. The trail is a three-mile round trip course over lava rock (wear proper shoes) and then up the cone. You'll hike across the lonely a'a lava flow, through spatter ramparts, fissures and lava tree molds. The lava tree molds are very interesting. Take time to look down into them.

I always feel an affinity for the straggly 'ohi'a trees and lava tree molds on each side of the path, which seem like sad and alien creatures stranded in a forbidding world. Mauna Ulu, "Growing Mountain," can be seen in the distance, a tall, still steaming, shield-shaped red mountain formed by numerous fierce eruptions along the volcanic rift zone just a few years ago.

Walk carefully as the lava ramparts here are sharp as razor blades. You will come to a field of pahoehoe lava, as smooth as the a'a was rough. Then you will hike up through a forested area, the kipuka, to Pu'u Huluhulu, a verdant oasis where lava has flowed all around but left this swath of land unscathed. The trail is narrow and steep, and switches-back eleven times before reaching the top.

Just before reaching the very top, if you watch carefully, you will see a short trail to the right. This is a good place to sit in the soft grass for a while and stare at Mauna Ulu. This is a nice spot for lunch or a snack, or also a wonderful place to meditate. Then continue up to the top. It's usually very windy up here, and chilly, so remember to take a parka or jacket. There's a marker pointed in various directions to the different landmarks. I love to sit and stare at Mauna Ulu from this vantage point.

Puu O'o, which is currently erupting lava, may be seen smoking and belching away, and sometimes you can faintly see the glow of the red molten lava that wounds down from O'o's flanks to the sea thirty miles away. Directly opposite to it, and much nearer, is Halema'uma'u, with its toxic plume rising majestically high into the sky. In early morning sunlight, it is colored light hues of orange, pink and blue. The peaks of Mauna Kea and Mauna Loa may be clear; massive Mauna Loa, Long Mountain, the second largest mountain in the solar system, looms across the Island from the north to the south like a colossal sleeping giant, and the tip of Mauna Kea can be shrouded in snow. You may see all the way across the Ka'u desert to the furthest tip of the Island, South Point.

Looking straight down, look into the heart of the cinder and spatter cone that was built by eruptions about 300 or more years ago. Birds twitter and fly from branches of trees that line the steep and inaccessible walls of the pit crater that has been spared the rivers of lava that have overrun the rest of the surrounding country. Look out over the frozen lava plain at the base of Pu'u Huluhulu, now the stunning and forbidding-looking remains of a huge lava lake, surrounded on all sides by a wall of lava twenty feet taller than the lake. When it erupted only forty years ago, it sent huge quantities of molten lava flowing in all directions, all the way to the ocean. Violent earthquakes rocked this area and a miles-long fissure opened, with fountaining over 200 feet in the air.

I love to sit and stare at Mauna Ulu. (Haven't I already told you that?) With the sunlight striking it, the heavy iron content of Mauna Ulu glows surreally red, and the incredible lava formations—escarpments and crevices and crags—appear like a stone citadel, made up of ornate and strangely decorated palaces and temples with giant walls, terraces and ramps. Sculptures and fantasies seem carved into ebony rock, and the frozen rivers and riverlettes of black lava seem still to course down the slopes, creating at one place a huge lake with its still frozen waves.

Mauna Ulu
(Growing Mountain)

*Take extreme caution in exploring Mauna Ulu. Wear appropriate footwear, take lots of water, and tread carefully!!! You are on your own out here. Sometimes there are no visitors around anywhere; they can't hear you if you get into trouble, and your cell phone may not work! Park Rangers will not encourage you to explore Mauna Ulu, and you should never go alone. At the very least, let someone know where you have gone, and report back to them after hiking to let them you know you are safe.

With that cautionary advice, I will say that that I hike Mauna Ulu often, but I always take great care!

The Mauna Ulu eruption of Kilauea began on May 24, 1969, and ended on July 22, 1974. At the time, Mauna Ulu was the longest flank eruption of any Hawaiian volcano in recorded history. The eruption created a new vent, covered massive amounts of land with lava, and added new land to the island.

There is no real trail to the top of Mauna Ulu! The slope is gentle but the lava is extremely fragile; several times, my feet have broken through some of the many shallow lava tubes. Listen carefully for the sound of hollow areas as you take each step; this area is famous for broken ankles, arms and legs. The ground crunches as you carefully step along the shell lava, the only sound to be heard in the stillness of this lava plain.

Steam and smoke are still coming out of the ground all around. You may choose to hike up through the huge channel where once a river of molten lava poured. The stinky smell of sulfur, like rotten eggs, becomes noticeable.

Finally, you will reach the top of the cone. Stop well before approaching the pit itself. You can see for miles in every direction, all the way to the sea. Black congealed lava spreads out for miles and glistens like black diamonds in the sunlight.

A huge crack completely around the summit of the cone, about ten feet from the edge, looks like it might break and collapse into the pit at any minute! What is at the bottom of that pit, and how far down it goes, no one knows, for the sides of the pit, almost a perfect circle, drop 180 degrees straight down into a blackness from which smoke unendingly spews in light wisps. Even hovering helicopters had been unable to photograph what is in the bottom of the pit, or if there is even a bottom. My heart pounds just to think of falling into that dark unknown.

I usually hike around counter clockwise, as if I am circumambulating the Kaaba Stone. Carefully skirt the threatening great crack! Admire the lava, which takes on a variety of hues—bright reds, browns, tans, grays, and blues. Great lava channels cut into the ground, and you will have to jump across some and scramble up and down others.

As you approach the other side of the cone, the scene completely changes. The jutted and razor-sharp turrets and spires of lava become flowing, swirling motifs and gingerbread gewgaws and fantastic giant imaginary animals. The graceful pahoehoe lava formations seem as if they are oddly frozen musical notations of some kind, and there is a hallucinatory power to the landscape, a Disneyland of frozen magma.

Napau Trail

This is a challenging 14-mile round trip trail that does require registration for day hiking. A permit is required if you plan to camp. These are both free. Just let the rangers know where you are. Rangers recommend a stock of at least three quarts of water per day for the hike. This trail is not suitable for small children.

This is a very dynamic, volcanically active area, erupting as recently as early winter 2011. That's recent! It can erupt again at any minute!

Follow the ahu, the rock piles, and stay on the trail. Watch your footing! The journey to Napau is seven miles one way over wild and truly fascinating landscape. Remember to keep your eyes on the ground as you walk. The trail skirts around the mouth of Makaopuhi Crater and eventually ends at Napau Camp, which has no water or shelter.

The trail continues from the bottom of Pu'u Huluhulu, and it is clearly marked. It passes under a "perch pond" on Mauna Ulu's side. After crossing Pu'u Huluhulu, it travels along the bed of a lava channel.

A strenuous three-mile trek across the desert passes an impressive rift from the Mauna Ulu eruption. Here you can see a good example of the start of a lava tube, before reaching the immense Makaopuhi Crater. Then you will hike up the Alae Shield, near the rim of the peak crater. The trail climbs down the Alae Shield and reaches Makaopuhi Crater. From here, the trail travels through rain forest. You will pass through 'Ohi'a trees and tree ferns in the forest; the rainforest will sometimes open up at places where lava has burned down the trees.

As you skirt around the west and then south side of Makaopuhi Crater, the path enters a forest of uluhe (false-staghorn fern), hapu'u and 'ohi'a trees, becoming more defined. Pleasant trekking through the forest, surrounded by twittering birds, gives some welcome shade from what can be piercing heat.

Pass the Kalapana trail on the right, and follow the main route as it swings gently northeast; it continues as a clearly defined trail through the forest. In three miles you come to a junction. Straight on (left) takes you further towards Pu'u 'O'o; at this time, this trail is closed. Take the right fork and you come to a dead end, the edge of the Napau Crater. A small clearing on the crater rim looks out across the crater with a great view of smoking Pu'u 'O'o. This overlook makes for a great lunch spot before returning by reverse route.

Continuing on Chain of Craters...

Ainahou Ranch

At mile 4.1 is the Ainahou Ranch, built in 1941 and listed on the National Register of Historic Places. This is one of my favorite places! However, check with the rangers to find out if is it open. During nene breeding season, it is closed. If it is open, you are in for a real treat, but you must hike a bit.

At approximately 4.2 miles you will see a sign and a right hand turn for the ranch. Make the right turn and you will come to a locked gate. Park off the road as much as you can. After you have parked your car, walk around the gate and simply go down the road. This is an easy walk approx. 2.7 miles one way. The ranch itself is not marked on the trail other than the sign on Chain of Craters Road showing the turnoff for the ranch,

After approximately one-half mile, you will encounter a split in the road. A trail sign tells you to take the left—the sign is *wrong*. Do *not* take the left fork; instead, take the right fork.

After having taken the *right* fork, you are now headed towards the ranch, which is still not visible. To the front and to the right of you are tall fir trees; these firs mark the start of the ranch itself. Keep along this road until you see another road branching to the right. Take this right branch and keep going. You are now entering the fir tree area. Round the curve and you will see the ranch.

This incredible ranch was built by H.C. Shipman as a haven against Japanese invasion during WWII. Shipman was very interested in wildlife conservation and one of the uses for the ranch was to provide protection for the endangered nene. Shipman was a cattle rancher—the original property was over 64,000 acres of pristine native forests and grasslands. The property is still home to nene and is not open to the public during the breeding season if nenes are found to be nesting in the area.

The 13.3-acre historic site sits within a native mesic forest at an elevation of 3000 feet. Within this forest, gardens surround a unique house creating an exotic setting that reflects Shipman's love of horticulture. He grew a vast collection of plants, which included orchids, orchards, a tree farm, and rare plants from around the world.

In 1971Shipman terminated his lease with B.P. Bishop Estate, at which point the National Park Service acquired it.

When you are ready to leave this lovely place, just retrace your path.

Back on Chain of Craters Road...

Muliwai a Pele viewpoint is about 7.4 miles down Chain of Craters Road. This viewpoint overlooks lava flows from 1969 and the 1969-74 eruptions from Mauna Ulu. Here the lava descends Holei Pali and continues towards the sea. The 1969 flow did not quite reach the sea, but the later flows did.

Kealakomo lookout is about 8.7 miles down Chain of Craters Road. A wooden hut perched on the side of the cliff will come into view. The handicapped-accessible Kealakomo is built on the Holei Pali and looks down over a 2,000 ft. drop to the ocean. The pavilion faces the direction of the Kealakomo Village, destroyed in a 1971 lava flow. This can be a great place for lunch, though usually windy. The Naulu Trail begins across the street. It eventually connects with the Napau Crater Trail to the north. It also intersects the unmaintained 10-hour Kalapana trail.

The pullout at Halona Kahakai is very near the crest of the Holei Pali fault escarpment. The road takes a dramatic hairpin turn that you should approach with caution. In another mile, the elevation will have dropped to 1,000 ft as you rapidly approach the coast.

For several hundred feet above and below Alanui Kahiko (Old Road) lookout, at approx. mile marker 13.7, can be seen remnants of the old Chain of Craters Road, buried under 300 feet of lava in the 1972 eruptions of Alae Lava shield flow.

At mile 14.9 is the Skylights Climb, a trail that leads up a hill with a hole in it—the Lava Tube Tumulus—where magma was once vented. I can't say I have tried this trail; if you are interested, ask for information at the Park Center.

Pu'u Loa, at approx. mile marker 15.9, is the largest concentration of ancient Hawaiian stone carvings in the State, perhaps in Polynesia, with more than 20,000 petroglyphs. Once you reach mile marker 15.9 you'll see two pullouts on either side of the road and a small park sign marking the start of the seven tenths of a mile petroglyph trail. This is a must stop!

Pu'u Loa Petroglyphs

The walk to Pu'u Loa takes you over an ancient field of pahoehoe lava with small scrubby plants pushing their way between the cracks. The path is well worn and marked by cairns of rock, as well as by its smoothness and discolorations, for untold numbers of feet have trod over this path for centuries. The park has built a boardwalk around some of the petroglyphs to protect the fragile carvings while still allowing visitors to enjoy them.

In Hawaiian, the petroglyphs are called ki'i pohaku, stone images. Their meaning is apparently lost, which seems to indicate that they are very ancient indeed.

Interestingly, petroglyphs do not occur throughout Polynesia. According to one authority, a line drawn from Hawaii to New Zealand divides the islands into those that have the strange drawings and those that do not—those east of the line are the isles with petroglyphs. This then, might indicate that their origin lies southeast, toward Easter Island, where petroglyphs and a written language existed prehistorically. Lots of room for conjecture here!

The petroglyphs consist of straight lines, semicircles, and concentric rings as well as strange stick figures of humans that are very powerfully emotive. There are also thousands of small pits drilled into the lava—it is commonly believed that the umbilical cords of newborn infants were buried here as a sacred practice.

There are also some who believe that the mysterious symbols are a form of divine communion known only by the kahunas, the priests. Still others believe that the petroglyph fields were genealogical record repositories. I have stood and looked at the petroglyphs of Puu Loa for hours, and whatever they are, they are certainly some kind of sacred record keeping. This is a place of mana, spiritual power. Do tread respectfully.

Interestingly, most of the human figures are males, but some of the groupings are obviously made of a man, woman, and child. Many of the figures are warrior figures; their helmets and weapons are clearly discernable, and their fighting stances are definitely intimidating. There are also drawings of canoes, fish, and lizards, and more rarely, symbols that seem to be the sun, moon and stars. I have never seen petroglyphs of flowers, which indicates to me that there is definitely something intrinsically masculine about them. I think they were drawn by men. Wouldn't women draw flowers?

It is forbidden by law to disturb the petroglyphs in any way. Please do not touch them or make rubbings. If the great rivers of lava of Goddess Pele have flowed all around them and spared them, certainly we can too. With that admonition, I will tell you about the petroglyphs that lie just on the other side of the small hill off the far side of the boardwalk.

Walk in a two o'clock direction from the boardwalk over the hill. You will be amazed and delighted by the thousands! of petroglyphs. Please tread lightly and very respectfully if you explore them; do not walk on them. Look up at the immense pali (cliff), with its broad, frozen rivers of lava, and then down again at the inexplicable stick drawing. You may get, as I do, a strange feeling for the sacredness of this spot and the mana it must have held for the ancients—a place where the indomitable forces of nature meet with the mind of man.

I like to meditate here during the intense heat of the day. What do I meditate upon? The puniness but courage of striving humankind in the face of the overwhelming forces of nature.

Be sure and bring lots of water if you do come here in the midday. It can be really hot!

Continuing on Chain of Craters Road…

Holei Sea Arch

Near the end of Chain of Craters Road is the Holei Sea Arch. To take in fully the enormous power of the volcano that you are driving on, pull over at mile marker 14.4. It is easy to see how the lava came pouring down in waves over the Holei Pali, forming gigantic rivers flowing down the Pali, and oozing its way to the ocean. Holei Pali (Pali means cliff) is the name of the 400-meter high escarpment along the Hilina fault system. Lava flowed from Mauna Ulu over the cliffs between 1969 and 1974. Whew!

Parking is available on either side of the road. On your right is the short trail to the ocean and a view of Holei Sea Arch.

Sea arches are formed when lava is continuously pounded by heavy surf until it is undercut in the shape of an arch. The cliffs are 80 to 90 feet high, but many waves still spray and wash over them, so use caution. Restrooms are available; well, let's call them, appropriately enough, "pit-stops."

Until just a few years ago, great molten rivers of fire coursed down the slopes of the Pali and cascaded into the sea here. At that time, every night hundreds of tourists parked here and walked out onto the lava fields to watch the hair-raising sight. The really intrepid ventured close enough to the molten lava to burn the soles of their shoes.

It was within site of the Holei Sea Arch that my friend Prem Nagar fell into the sea of fire when an earthquake broke off the lava shelf upon which he was standing. His last words were, according to his friend who ran for dear life when he felt the quake, and survived, "Give me a show, mama." She did.

This is the end of Chain of Craters Road. Turn around, drive slowly, and admire the majesty of this incredible place.

A Hidden Place Within the Park (Shhh!)...
Pua Po'o
(Cock's Comb Cave; The Wild Cave)

Pua Po'o, "Cock's Comb Cave," called sometimes "The Secret Cave" and sometimes "The Wild Cave," is a pristine lava cave discovered just a few years ago when Park workers were putting in a pig fence. You won't find it on any Park maps because its location is kept a secret. In the past, one day a week, a ranger led twelve lucky people, and only twelve, through this very special ecological treasure, and it was free! That's all changed though.

It's a five-mile round hike (allow 6 hours) through the rain forest, and before descending down a ladder into the cave, the guide will ask everyone on the tour to promise not to disclose its location. Everyone is required to wear helmets with headlamps and leather gloves, which are provided. Also it is a requirement to wear long pants and closed toes shoes. Pack a snack, too. Water, of course.

As of now, until June 2016, the cost is $175 for adults, and $75.00 for youth (7-12). You do get lunch now, a commemorative souvenir (?) and a Certificate of Completion. **Reservations are required and can only be made via Friends of Hawaii Volcanoes National Park website**. For reservation information, current prices, and dates and times, here is the website: http://www.fhvnp.org/institute/wild-caves-exploration/ Please note that the tours are not offered on a set schedule, they are very popular, so make your reservation early!

What's so special about this cave? It's pristine, the way Nahuku probably used to be before it was discovered. Golden and silver lava icicles and lava stalagmites by the tens of thousands hang from the ceiling; the walls have untold numbers of niches with natural altars which turn the whole cave into a glittering cathedral.

The walls of the cave are coated with beautiful, mottled, whitish-colored bacteria giving one the impression of strange prehistoric art; this bacterium is currently being researched as a cancer cure. It is as much for this reason as protection that the leather gloves are required. It is strictly forbidden to touch the walls of the cave, in order not to contaminate it.

The cave is entered through a "skylight." A skylight is made when a small section of a tube roof collapses. Hikers must climb down a 15-foot ladder into the tube, scramble over slippery, sharp rocks, and walk about 25 feet in a crouched position over uneven surfaces. One must scramble over rocks and boulders to navigate through the cave, and getting out of the tube again is a fairly rough, scrambling climb. It is not a suitable excursion for small children or the elderly.

Pua Po'o is named for a stalagmite curiously shaped like a rooster's crest—a fin-shaped piece of lava with a series of small horizontal spikes. There are several of these odd formations; scientists have yet to figure out how they were formed.

The rangers who lead this tour are very knowledgeable, and present a fascinating glimpse into one of the least known ecosystems in the world, the lava tube, with its blind spiders and blind crickets.

I never get enough of going down into this wonderful world; it always fills me with awe. If you want to experience this magical place, dial that phone at exactly 7:45 and keep hitting that redial button!

Sandalwood Trail and Kilauea Caldera Hike
A great hike! (2.5 hours)

Since Halema'uma'u's plume has been going off for almost four years, the trails down in Kilauea Crater have been off-bounds, except for this one, which skirts the bottom of Kilauea's cliffs. This is a lovely trail through a sulfur steam-vent area, with spectacular caldera views; it descends through rain forest down into the crater, up again into rainforest and then leads along the old Crater Rim Road. It does pass through the Sulfur Banks, so if you have respiratory problems, small children, or if you are pregnant, it probably is not for you. It is moderately difficult.

This hike begins at the Park Center. Walk past the Center, cross the street on the same side, and take the paved sidewalk. You will see the Volcano Art Gallery a short distance away over on your right, and closer on your right you will see a large sculpture. Take a moment to look at it.

In 2004, Hawaii Volcanoes National Park issued a call to artists for proposals to create a sculpture portraying the concept of "wahi kahu," or sacred place. "Ulumau Pohaku Pele," "Forever Growing, the Rock of Pele," by Kona artist Kalewa Matsushita, is meant to remind visitors that Hawaii Volcanoes National Park is a place of natural and scientific wonders, and also a place that is sacred to Native Hawaiians. The sculptor said he drew inspiration from a kupuna, a Hawaiian elder, who envisioned the sculpture in a dream.

Just a short distance further on the trail, toward your right, you will see the hula platform, Ka 'Ulu o Laka (the inspiration of Laka, the hula goddess). Here is where traditional hula and chant is performed. If you look to your left, you will see why this spot was chosen; the view of Kilauea from here is superb. Behind the hula platform is a reconstruction of a traditional thatched hale (house) where the hula dancers gather before and after their performance. Go off trail and have a look. I wouldn't mind living in a house like this, would you?

After you take a look, get back on the trail and descend down this lovely walkway bounded by a cliff on the right. This is the Sulfur Banks Trail.

As you come out of the shaded wooded area, the trail becomes a boardwalk and the view opens up expansively. Huge cliffs on the right mark the outer Kilauea Crater edge; there is a signboard at the bench that explains some of the geological characteristics of this area. It's quite fascinating, really. Ahead of you in the distance is the great Mauna Loa. I like to sit for a while at this bench and enjoy the panoramic view.

As the path continues along, you will know you are closer and closer to sulfur vents by the smell, the delightful whiff of rotten eggs. You may want to hold your breath at times. Look toward your right at the beautiful sulfur banks; you will see deposits of minerals on the rocks. The bright yellow is sulfur. There is a sign describing the formation of mineral deposits in this area.

Do not get off the trail. These vents are hot and you could be seriously burned.

The path continues to meander along through Sulfur Banks. See my description above of Sulfur Banks, for further information on this area.

At the end of this walkway, you will come to the highway. Cross it, and continue straight ahead until you reach a trail junction. The one we will take is the middle trail. It has a sign that reads "Sandalwood Trail," ("lliahi Trail").

There is another access to this trail just to the side of Volcano House, but I prefer this route.

You will descend down past a grotto of huge ferns that look like Boston ferns; they are not but they are closely related. If it's a cold day, you can stop at this grotto and get warm; there are steam vents here, which is why the ferns grow so luxuriantly. A short distance further, you will come to a superb overlook of Kilauea caldera. To your left, if in season (late summer and early fall), you may find some strawberry guavas. Sample them; they are considered invasive, but save some for me!

Keep descending. You may wonder where the sandalwood trees are. Unless you are an expert, you won't find them. There are not too many, but there are some very young ones right on the trail.

The story of the demise of the great sandalwood forests, which is part of the near demise of the Hawaiian people, is tragic. You might want to read about it.

Half way to the caldera, you will come to a fork in the trail. There is a bench here, and this is a lovely place to rest for a few moments and listen to the forest birds.

When you are ready to move on, take the path that descends down. You will amble now through a Himalayan ginger forest. This ginger is invasive, one of the most invasive plants in the Park, but just the same, the blossom of this plant is incredibly otherworldly. It is called "kahili ginger" in Hawaiian, named for the great feathered kahili standards used by Hawaiian royalty. The blossoms are as large as 18 inches, and fantastically fragrant. Even though it's a terrible pest, this trail is wonderfully fragrant during ginger season, which is late summer through fall.

You will pass huge many-ton boulders carpeted with damp moss. Look up toward your left to see where they came from!

After a short climb up and then down again, and you will descend all the way to the caldera.

At the end of the descent, take the path to the left. There will be a sign saying that that path straight ahead is closed. That path goes toward the plume. You don't want to take it!

Almost immediately after turning left, you will enter the caldera. It is marked by ahu, stone cairns.

Look up to your left. If you look closely, you will see an overlook; that's where you will be later during this hike. Take your time along the lava trail and admire the scintillating, iridescent colors of the lava. I love the crunch, crunch sound as I walk along here.

To your right is Halema'uma'u. This is as close to Pele's home as you can legally get.

I like to go off trail a little to the left, climb up on one of the big boulders, bask in the sun, and admire the view.

The climb out of the caldera is, predictably, kind of steep. There are some great views of the caldera just after you begin to climb out. Be sure to turn and look back a few times.

When you reach the junction of Crater Rim Trail, there is a bench. Again, this is a lovely place to sit and listen to birds. Then take the path to the left.

Keep hanging straight ahead, and you will eventually begin to climb again. When the trail gets a little steep, you will come to a landfall with some big boulders. This was a landfall that happened during an earthquake of the 1970's; several people camping in one of the Park campsites were killed by the tsunami triggered by this quake. (Things do happen!) There is a great view of Kilauea caldera from here.

When you come to the next junction, pause at the iron railing for the view. For some reason, this is a place that the birds love, and it is easy to spot them from below, flitting about from tree limb to tree limb.

Take the path to the left, which begins to ascend. The other path goes to Kilauea I'ki overlook. In less than a half-mile, you will go across a paved road where the trail picks up again. In a short distance, you will come to the old Crater Rim Road. You will know it by the jungle plants growing through its potholes and earthquake cracks.

Walk along this road a short distance. When you see a part of the road curving left, take this to another great view of Kilauea Crater. There are a couple of picnic tables here right on the edge of the Crater where you can sit and take it all in.

When you are ready to continue, just walk along the road ahead and it will curve back to the old road on your left. Amble along; it will take you back to the Park Center.

Hope you enjoyed this beautiful, multi-terrain walk.

My Favorite Long Day Hike

This is an eight-mile loop that includes one of my favorite wooded areas, the Enchanted Forest. You won't find "Enchanted Forest" on any of the Park maps—that's what it is called by some of the locals.

It's a section of Crater Rim Trail. Not many people hike it; in fact, I have rarely encountered anyone else in the Enchanted Forest.

This hike is moderately difficult but does require some stamina. This is the hike I like to take my friends on. If you have five to six hours and want to do a hike you will remember, a hike that pretty much has it all, this is the one. Bring lunch or a snack, water, and a flashlight. Also, bring light raingear. One never knows.

Begin at the Kilauea I'ki lookout. Take the path toward Thurston Lava Tube (toward the left, as you face the crater). Hike one-half mile to Thurston and then descend down into the crater. Do all the things that people do down in the Crater, and then ascend back up on the far side. It's a mile across. After you ascend the steep steps (did I say steep?), take the first path upward **immediately to the left** (in the opposite direction from the bench you will see). Sometimes this path is overgrown with grasses, so you may have to look closely. Of course, you might want to rest on the bench for a few minutes. That was a steep climb!

Walk a short distance, about an eighth of a mile, and turn left at the junction. You will pass through a gate (please close it again behind you; it protects from pigs) and in about ten steps, if you look closely, you will see a sort of footpath to the right. Follow it a few steps to the edge of Kilauea Caldera; this is a great view. There is a log you can sit on and admire Halema'uma'u. **Be careful not to fall in!**

Retrace your steps to the trail and follow it about a quarter of a mile until it forks to the left. (You can no longer go straight ahead; the Park has closed that portion of the trail because of Halema'uma'u's plume). Note how the terrain changes; it becomes much dryer and is not as lush.

As you emerge out of the forest, you will see Pu'u Pua'i ahead. Hike up and up the red cinder hill, but stop at the top of Desolation Peak and sit and admire the breathtaking view of Mauna Loa, Mauna Kea, and Kilauea Caldera.

At the top, take a leisurely stroll through this area. You may see nene, because this is one of their favorite feeding areas. This is an ecological regeneration area; as you can see by the bleached tree bones, it was devastated by the 1959 eruption of Kilauea I'ki.

Though the red ground cover you see everywhere is lovely, it is an invasive weed, fireweed. Still lovely, though. You may also see blackberries; eat them. They too are invasive.

When you get to the parking lot, turn left and take the paved path up Devastation Trail to another Kilauea I'ki overlook, one-half mile. There is a picnic table here and this is a great place to have lunch and rest. You are now halfway!

After lunch, retrace your path the half-mile to the parking lot. You'll see lots you didn't see the first time. If you look carefully, you may see a few tree molds just off the path.

At the parking lot, turn left and head across it. You will be going opposite to the direction from which you earlier came. Cross the road (Chain of Craters Road) and walk along the road on the left side about one-eighth of a mile. You will see a sign on the left that says "Crater Rim Trail." Take this trail; it leads into the Enchanted Forest. (There is also a "Crater Rim Trail" sign on the right hand side of the road—you want to go left).

The Enchanted Forest is a two-mile hike up a very gradual slope, through a lovely hapu'u forest with many native plants, especially a large collection of various ferns. When I take people into this forest, I ask that we hike in silence. And you may want to be silent too.

Why silent? So that you may experience the rain forest in all of its mystery and magic. Creaking limbs, whispering and sighing breezes, chirping, trilling, rare songbirds, the gurgling of shy kalesh fowls and the Om of swordtail crickets delight the ears. The giant tree ferns, many 30 feet tall, wave their delicate, feathery fronds in the breezes, touching you gently as if blessing you as you pass along the path beside them. Rare endemic plants surround you at every turn in the trail—stag horn ferns, wild orchids... thimbleberry and wild strawberry abound.

This is the gentle woodland garden realm of Laka, the beautiful goddess of the forest. Nature spirits are alive and well here! Walk in silence and awe through a forest that once only bird catchers and sacred herb gatherers walked in solitude, and if you are attuned, you may feel how the ancients must have felt walking through this sacred ground—respectful, appreciative, and with tenderness. Take your time to enjoy and drink in the magic and mystery of this pristine forest.

At the end of the forest trail, you will see a sign, "Crater Rim Trail." Turn left, and begin the walk up this wide, old trail way. It is now called Escape Road, but it was used by the ancients for centuries. At the top, after about a half-mile hike, open the gate and in a few steps you will arrive at your last stop, Nahuku Crater, with its 1500-foot long lava tube cave, Thurston Lava Tube.

The first section of the 600 feet cave is artificially lit, but the last portion, with its eerie dark entrance, looks foreboding. This portion is now closed, due to the ceiling falling. See the section on Nahuku for more info.

After exploring Nahuku, cross the street, turn right and it's one-half mile back to our starting point, Kilauea I'ki overlook. A truly magical, mystical tour through eons of evolutionary time!

******

Great Places Outside the Gated Park
(but still in the Park)…

Mauna Loa Road
(The Strip)

The Mauna Loa Strip Road, called fondly "the Strip," connects the main part of Hawaii Volcanoes National Park at the summit of Kilauea with the upper elevations of Mauna Loa. You can drive toward the summit of Mauna Loa on the Mauna Loa Strip Road for spectacular views at the road's end.

It climbs and winds from 4000 to the 6700 feet elevation, approximately ten miles, and above that Mauna Loa Trail continues to Red Hill cabin on the East rift zone, and then to the summit of Mauna Loa.

In the past, the Strip was used for cattle and horse pasture and infested with feral goats and sheep. It is still degraded habitat, infested with pasture grasses and weeds, but it is also home for many rare native plants and animals. In recent years, the Park has been restoring the Strip's habitats.

The last kipuka is at the end of Strip Road. Beyond is increasingly-sparse scrub forest and lava fields. The Mauna Loa Summit Trail begins at the end of the road.

All the common native forest birds are found in the area. If you are a bird watcher, you might want to hike up the Strip. Walking along the Strip in the evening, with the sometimes-magnificent view of the sea, is very rewarding.

Also, note that occasionally the Strip is closed due to fire hazard. There will be a sign if this is the case.

Local cyclists like to struggle up this road, and then feel as if they are flying on the way down. This is a good place to walk the dog also, but keep them leashed, please. Nenes live here.

Tree Molds

To get to Tree Molds, take Highway 11 approximately 2.5 miles west, toward Kona, to Mauna Loa Road, which will be on the mauka (mountainside) side of the road. You can walk the loop road or drive it. This short excursion just takes minutes and is well worth the time.

Here you will see tree molds that formed when pahoehoe lava (the smooth, ropey lava) poured through the deep tropical forest. The trees were too wet to burn, resisting bursting into flames just long enough for the lava to cool around the trunks. (Seems unlikely to me, but I've been assured that's how it happened.) When the trees rotted, unusual, deep pit molds were left behind for our enjoyment.

There is a difference between what are called lava trees and lava tree molds. Lava trees form when still-fluid lava flows away, leaving a freestanding shell composed of lava that solidifies in contact with a tree. Lava tree molds form when lava solidifies in place around a tree.

Peer inside the molds, and look at the interesting impressions the trees left.

Kipuka Puaulu
(Bird Park)

Bird Park is also outside of the gated entrance, two miles from the Park entrance toward Kona. Turn mauka (toward the mountain) on Mauna Loa road to the parking area for Kipuka Puaulu. A kipuka, an area of land spared by lava flows, because of its isolation may become, in time, an evolutionarily unique biosystem. You may not see as many birds as you hear, but you will definitely hear them. Besides the natives, you may see exotic birds (in this case, exotic means birds other than our native birds) such as the house finch, northern cardinal, Japanese white-eye, kalij pheasant, melodious laughing-thrush, and red-billed leiothrix.

This is a peaceful place to have a picnic, and there are tables here. Eat your lunch in this wonderfully fragrant forest amid rare birds singing their hearts out. Kipuka Puaulu is one of the few places easily accessible to the public where you still stand a chance of seeing either of the two living native butterflies, the Kamahameha and the Koa butterfly. You'll also find native plants typical of the mesic forest growing here, as Bird Park is now a protected area. It also is a collection of some of the rarest trees on Earth, including Ochrosea haleakalae, Sapindus saponaria, and giant koa.

The one-mile loop can be driven or walked.

Namakani Paio

Namakani Paio means "the conflicting winds," and this is an appropriate name for this lovely oasis of a camp-and-picnic ground, with its stately and fragrant groves of giant eucalyptus trees, for it often is windy, though usually pleasantly so.

It can be easily accessed by car about three miles west of the Park entrance, that is, toward Kona; it is well marked. It is free to camp here and you do not have to pay to enter. No reservations are required; it is first-come, first served, though I have rarely seen many people here, thankfully. There are also small cabins for rent but at the time of this writing, these are not available. Ask at the Park for availability. There are restrooms, barbecue grills, and a covered pavilion. During dry periods, fires are prohibited.

Namakani can also be accessed from a footpath directly across from Jaggar Museum within the Park. It takes about fifteen minutes to walk it.

This is a jewel of a place. I don't know who planted the now-giant eucalyptus trees, but I am forever grateful. I love to picnic here, a quick drive from Volcano Village, and it is so wonderful to lie in the soft grass, listen to the sound of rare birds and the wind in the leaves, and just imbibe the healing scent of the eucalyptus. It is at 4000 feet, the very crest of Kilauea, so if you do camp, please know that it can be damp and chilly, so plan accordingly.

This is a great place to bring children too. There are short trails to climb and open expanses to play in.

Namakani has a feeling of safety and serenity. Do try to experience it, even if you just drive in with your windows down to breath in the aromatic fragrance for a few moments.

Ka'u Desert Footprints

Footprints fossilized in the Ka'u Desert ash hold a mystery, and know one really knows the answer, but there is a fascinating story around them that preserves an important event in ancient Hawaiian history.

There are two footprint-bearing ash layers in the desert, each separated by 90 cm of dune sand. The footprints can be found heading in both a northeasterly and southwesterly direction.

They were discovered in 1919 by accident. Who made these bare footprints, and when? How is it they are preserved?

The story is that they were made by a group of warriors and their families, led by Keoua, the enemy of Kamehameha, as they made their way back to their home in the district of Ka'u, after an indecisive battle for the sovereignty of the island. The weary group camped on Kilauea at a sacred heiau (temple) to Pele, and then split up into three groups for the march across the desert.

The first party made it safely across. But as the second party was midway across, Kilauea erupted, volcanic ash and hot gas exploded from the caldera, and a thick cloud of ash, sand and rocks was ejected out of the crater and rained down for miles around.

When the third party, not in the path of the ash cloud, finally gathered themselves together and marched onward, they saw ahead of them their people lying upon the ground apparently resting. As they drew closer however, they realized that they were all dead.

The story tells that husbands and wives and children lay entwined together, their noses touching, which is the way the ancients communicated their love. Only one pig escaped death. Estimates of the number of fatalities range from about 80 to 5,405. The year was said to be1790.

Hawaii volcanologists who have examined the mystery tell that rather than a dense ash cloud, the unlucky warriors and their families were killed by a "pyroclastic surge," a stream of hurricane force winds, composed of hot steam and sulfuric gases.

This event had huge consequences for Hawaiian history. Keoua interpreted this tragic event as a sign that Goddess Pele had abandoned him, and soon after, surrendering himself hopelessly to his fate, he became the first human sacrifice at the great war heiau built by Kamehameha.

Recently archeologists have found evidence that there were temporary dwellings here in this very arid place, which says a lot for the physical stamina and resourcefulness of the ancient people. After all, what did they do for water?

Archeologists believe that they came here to chip away at the lava rock, collecting fragments for their tools. Some archeologists have theorized that many of the footprints in the desert, rather than being the footprints of the ill-fated warriors, are the footprints of these people, mostly women and children for some reason, which would account for their small size.

An easy hike begins at the desert trailhead eight miles south of the park entrance on Highway 11, between mile markers 37 and 38. The entrance is clearly marked; there's an emergency phone there. The trail is less than two miles roundtrip. Follow the part-sand, part-gravel path southeast away from the parking area; it isn't hard to follow.

You will reach a pavilion that protects some of these footprints. Unfortunately, they are weathered and have been vandalized. However, further out into the desert, sometimes covered by shifting sands, sometimes not, are thousands of well-preserved footprints.

If the tragic story of Keonehelelei, "the falling sands," captivates your imagination, you might want to do some exploring further into the desert from the pavilion. There are some beautiful rolling sand dunes with great vistas in every direction. Sunset, sitting on the dunes facing Mauna Loa, can be incredible, especially during full moon. There's an unspoiled loneliness about this place. My friends and I sometimes trudge in with our guitars and ukuleles, find a comfortable hollow in the dunes, and chant to the Great Spirit. It's that kind of place.

However, I would suggest you have a GPS receiver or get a guide—try volcanohawaiitour.com. If you have a very good sense of direction, it's doable during the day. But you could easily lose your way back at night. There are no trails through sand dunes.

There are many more footprints hidden in these dunes, some say thousands, and they are much better preserved; I have discovered some of these and it is thrilling to follow them a distance and imagine whose they were. The shifting sands of the desert, however, alternately cover these over and expose them again; once seen, they may never be seen again. Be sure to take plenty of water if you go exploring; it can get quite hot out here.

'Ola'a Forest and Pu'u Maka'ala

Pu'u Maka'ala, (Stay-Alert Hill), named for a cinder cone rising over 200 feet, is part of the much larger 'Ola'a Forest Reserve. 'Ola'a Forest is not contiguous with the rest of Hawaii Volcanoes

National Park. It is composed of two adjacent tracts of land separated by Wright Road.

Formerly called La'a, this elfin-like forest was a legendary place for collecting bird feathers. It was established to protect some of the Big Island's most important wet native forest and unique geologic features and it is an important habitat for some of Hawaii's rarest birds, as well as rare plants—there are 21 rare plants and four rare birds living here.

Access is 4.8 miles above Highway 11 just past mile marker 27, where you turn on Wright Road. Follow Wright Road toward the mountain, and then turn right on Amamau Road and follow until you reach the cul-de-sac. Then drive or park and walk the grassy trail one-fourth mile to the trailhead. You will see a sign and steps to climb over the fence.

This area is open to the public, but not encouraged for hiking by the Park for several reasons. Firstly, it is very possible to get thoroughly lost here; trails are not maintained, few people hike here, and the forest is dense and provides few clues to direction or location—everything begins to look alike. Lava tubes and cracks lace the entire area, and falling in one could be deadly. Pig hunters also may be in the area, and you might be mistaken for dinner. Secondly, this is some of the most pristine native forests in Hawaii, abundant with endemic plants and animals. Coming in here with seeds of weeds on your clothing or shoes could be fatal to many of these species, not to mention the dire effects of trampling upon them.

If you do come here, do not come alone. Best would be to have a GPS or come with a guide. A cell phone might work. Might not too. Bring rain gear and warm clothing for sure! And boots would be a plus. You're sure to get wet feet here.

This enchanting land is protected by Ku-ka-ʻohiʻa-Laka, the guardian god of the ʻohiʻa forests, Ua-kuahine, the goddess of the rains in ʻOlaʻa; and Ku-lili-ka-ua, the god of the thick mists that envelop the forests. In olden times, travel through this land was accompanied by prayer and care. Traditions tell us that many a careless traveler found themselves lost in a maze of overgrowth and dense mists because of disrespectful and careless actions.

The name "ʻOlaʻa" connotes sacredness and sanctity; the root of the name being "laʻa," which means "light." An ancient mele (chant) celebrating ʻOlaʻa sings:

> *The birds fly like flaming darts to the*
> *uplands of ʻOlaʻa,*
> *Where the mist and smoke darken*
> *the forest,*
> *Spread out by the breeze which lays out*
> *the blossoms,*
> *Man is like q flower, roving about...*
> *Something that is irreplaceable...*

The lands of the upper ʻOlaʻa region were remote even to the ancient Hawaiians. It was most frequently accessed by bird collectors (for feathers), canoe builders, and collectors of other unique items for which the region was famed.

These lands are classified as rain forest, with nearly 100 percent native plants. There are alien weeds at the edges of the forest, but once you are in the forest, 90 percent of the plants are endemic to Hawaii, and found nowhere else in the world. The forest is dominated by 20 to 30 foot-tall tree ferns called hapu'u, the largest ferns on Earth. These massive ferns have fallen, and tangled trunks and dead fronds make hiking off of the trail nearly impossible. One of the loveliest times to hike here is in spring, when the hapu'u fiddlehead fronds are unfurling; they seem to me to be some kind of benevolent aliens.

One surprise here is the giant nai'o, the" bastard sandalwood." When the sandalwood trade began to collapse in the mid-1800's due to greedy over-harvesting on the part of the ali'i, the bastard sandalwood nai'o was sometimes fraudulently supplied instead — hence its name. There are also giant koa here.

'Apapane, 'Oma'o, 'Elepaio and I'iwi are the four rare birds that abound here. If you're really in to identifying native plants and birds, this is THE best place to find them growing and flying wild in Hawaii. It will be worth your while to buy an identification guide or download one from the Internet.

Again, do take caution in this forest!

And now...
Volcano Village

Ah! Lovely, storybook pretty Volcano Village!

An old hamlet of winding, forested lanes and beguiling cottages right outside Hawaii Volcanoes

National Park. At nearly 4,000 feet, Volcano Village is much cooler and rainier than the coastal areas, so pack warmly.

Here you will find accommodations (there are roughly 200 bed and breakfasts, inns, and guesthouses), eateries, and some shopping.

A perfect place to live! At least, that's what all of us who live here think.

Summer day temperatures average 75 degrees Fahrenheit and winter temperatures hover around 65 degrees. Of course, with all the rain, over 150 inches per year, the temperature can drop, and often does, considerably lower at times. Most people here treasure their fireplaces. Fog and mist roll in most afternoons and evenings; these are quintessential Volcano scenarios. Volcano Village is kind of like a cross between an alpine village and Scotland.

An abundance of flowers, ferns, and rare birds make this paradise.

Like hydrangeas? This is hydrangea heaven during spring and summer. Never will you have seen such huge blossoms!

This is also probably the safest village in the world; you can walk the unlit streets and lanes at night without a care. In fact, just walking around is one of the enjoyments of this perfect village. Don't even worry about Kilauea erupting; since we're upslope of the crater, we're safer than most other areas of the Island. Five hundred years ago, this area was covered with extensive lava flows, but since then, the summit has reshaped itself and flows occur on the southern flank of the Volcano, away from the Village.

Sound confident, don't I?

Things to Do

The Village seems to be a sleepy little place, but behind the scenes, things may be bustling. Some of the best artists in Hawaii live here, and they are always getting reading for shows. Painters, sculptors, fabric artists, quilt makers, jewelers...you name the art, we have an expert. Pick up a free community newspaper in the upper general store (the one next to the post office). Here you will find art happenings and many other events.

If you like art and you happen to be here during the Thanksgiving weekend, lucky you! The Village is renowned for its Art Walk, a time when Village artists open up their studio homes and sell their wares for discounted prices. Some of their homes are something like out of Architectural Digest; just to visit, talk art, and see their pads is great fun.

One of the first things to do in the Village is visit Niaulani Campus, which is an adjunct of The Volcano Art Center. It's located on the main drag just a block south of the post office. You can't miss it. It's open Monday through Friday.

Among other things, they have a guided one-hour nature walk on Monday mornings (free), but you can go any time on your own. Amble through a natural eight-acre forest with no alien pests just to see what the Garden of Eden was really like. They also have concerts, often with world-class musicians, lectures by Hawaiian elders and storytellers, and many other events. They have a library in the "Great Room" where you can just sit by the fire and read. Check out their website, www.volcanoartcenter.org

for all their wonderful events. They have a bulletin board too just outside the building where you can find out about upcoming events.

On the only "main" street in town, Old Volcano Highway, you will find the post office, two general stores, a hardware store, and a laundry. The "Upper Store," the Volcano Store, sells all kinds of paraphernalia, including flashlights and raingear, as well as homemade Japanese food, such as a "scoop a' rice." They also sell beautiful cut flowers and anthuriums. The Kilauea General Store, one block down the street, has a great coffee bar and tasty locally made pastries. You can also buy firewood here. Both stores sell spirits (you know the kind), and both have gas pumps.

You may see a sandwich board just in front of our quaint Village Post Office (the cutest post office in the U.S.) on our "Main Street" (Old Volcano Road.) This is one of the ways we announce community events. You may see a sign for our Fourth of the July Parade, a real hoot, as some would say. Almost everyone and their dog (literally) in Volcano are in the parade. Don't miss it if you are in town on the Fourth. It's followed by an arts-and-crafts fair, a great silent auction, music, and lots of food venders at Cooper Center. It's like an old-fashioned, traditional Fourth.

Another event not to be missed, and also advertised by our post-office sandwich board, is the Mongolian barbecue. This is so popular we have it several times a year. It's all you can eat at the Cooper Community Center for just a few dollars—proceeds (nope, not a misprint!) Restaurant, my favorite eatery, which I will describe later. It also sells some local art in go to Cooper Center. Great Desserts!

Directions to Cooper Center—just turn up Wright Road off "Main Street." You can't miss it.

Cooper Center also features a "world class" skateboard rink. Wander on over and be amazed at some of the talented young skateboard masters.

There are a lot of cottage industries in the Village. All those artists have to have a way to earn a living! The Kilauea Store sells some of their products. They are usually right up front on the counter. Try "Holly's Dressing."

The hardware store is behind the Thai Thai restaurant. In front of Thai Thai is a tourist info center; you can get brochures here for various island activities. There is also a laundry in the back of the building.

A great place to shop is the little Kilauea Kreations shop, just behind the "General Store," adjacent to the Thai Thai Restaurant. It has one of the greatest selections of Hawaiian fabric on the Island; that's because a lot of quilters live in the Village. They have some fine examples of quilts hanging on the walls. You can find a good selection of local art here also. The number is 967-8090. Highly recommended!

Another place to pick up some nice gifts is at Birgitta Frazier's pottery studio, Da Raku Barn. It's on the corner of Wright Road and "Main Street." She's usually open. Just park and holler!

Harrowhawk Studios is owned by talented painter and metalworker Patrick Daniel Sarsfield.

It's right in the center of the Village and he's open by appointment. His number is 985-9934.

If you are here on a Sunday, you really are in luck. That's because it's THE day for the Village. It's the day when everyone comes out of the woodwork for the Farmer's Market. Don't miss it!

You will find everything from readymade, homemade food—Hawaiian, Japanese, Chinese, Mexican, Thai, Filipino, vegetarian—to flowers, art, puppies, locally grown vegetables, locally grown coffee and teas… you name it; you will find it. There are also several venders selling homemade breads and pastries. The fresh bread venders are the best!

There also is a thrift store with sometimes-great bargains, and a bookstore where books are just fifty cents. Most everyone has breakfast here—feasting on pancakes, pastries, tamales…because… the Market begins at six a.m. That's right! Six in the morning! It only lasts until about nine, so get there early. Sometimes there are Hawaiian musicians and hula dancers.

The Market is THE social event of the town. If there is anyone you are looking for, or information of any kind you seek, this is the place to go. We love our market. (I do all my shopping there, and only go to Hilo once a month!). It's located on Wright Road, which is just off the main drag, Old Volcano Highway. Look for the Cooper Center Community Center; you can't miss it; just follow the people.

Speaking of Cooper Center. This is the place where community activities go on. You can find yoga, tai chi, Hawaiian Huna, elder activities, whatever! Look in our newspaper (again, you can get one at the Kilauea Store) or check out the bulletin boards at Cooper Center. The Thrift Store is open weekdays from nine to twelve; you can often find some true treasures among the castoffs. And if you need high-speed Internet, you can sit in the arcade and surf away. There is also a playground for children, and as previously mentioned, the skateboard rink is located here.

In spite of the multitude of guest lodging places, they often fill up quickly. Look online before you come and make your reservation. Just google *Volcano Village Hawaii*. You'll find plenty, but book early, especially during the winter season. The best deal in town is Volcano Places. Gracious Kathryn Grout offers your choice of several accommodations, featuring the woodwork of notable craftsman Kenneth Lahte. Her number is 895-7470.

If you're traveling on a limited budget, we even have a youth hostel, the Holoholo Inn. The number is 808-967-8025 or 808-967-7950.

Feel like some body work while you're here? Suzanna Valerie, 896-5661, is a licensed massage therapist. For acupuncture, call Eve de Molin at 985-8699.

If you're in the Church-going mood, we have the KMC Chapel, telephone 967-7315, the Volcano Assembly of God, telephone 967-8191, and New Hope Christian Fellowship, telephone 967-7129 Buddhist meditation is offered as well. Call 985-7470 for more information

Like to golf? One of the most unusual courses in the world is right down the road, The Volcano Golf Course. The often mist-shrouded course may remind you of playing in Scotland. Isn't that where golf began? Take the Mauna Loa Road just a half-mile from the Park entrance, toward Kona. They have a restaurant that is open for lunch daily; they serve huge portions for the money, which makes a lot of locals happy. The number is 967-8228. The golf shop number is 967-7331.

Just down the road from the golf course is the Volcano Winery. They make their wine from their own grapes! They have free wine tasting. Try the Mac Nut Honey wine. Not for connoisseurs perhaps but tasty in a local sort of way. Their number is 967-7479.

One place you won't want to miss is Akatsuka Gardens. Just beyond the 23-mile marker, traveling toward Hilo, with free entrance, you will see more beautiful orchids in one place than you have seen in your life. The most exotic too. Do take your camera. They don't mind if you spend hours photographing their beautiful, otherworldly orchids. You can also buy orchids and anthuriums and ship them home. The staff is very knowledgeable and very friendly.

You might or might not be surprised to know how many people choose Kilauea volcano for the place to scatter their loved one's ashes. If this appeals to you, call 800-908-9764 or locally call 808-967-8617.

Ah! Places to eat! The most important thing of all!

If you don't mind dropping some dollars, Kilauea Lodge is the premier place to dine. Featuring continental cuisine, you will enjoy the ambiance of the big old fireplace, the art on the walls, the lovely decorated tables. Desserts are great! You might need reservations for dinner. The number is 967-7366. Dress is casual. But you can also dress up.

The Lodge also serves lunch, and they have really great lunch specials for around ten dollars. Try the grilled cheese sandwich with fries. It's so big, you will have half of it to take home for dinner.

The Lava Rock Cafe is also very popular with locals and tourists alike. They are inexpensive and also serve huge portions (seems that's what people expect here?) and have a very extensive menu. They serve breakfast and lunch. It's a cute and friendly place. They also have wonderful homemade desserts. Try the pumpkin crunch. Their number is 967-8526. Reservations are not needed, unless you have a big party.

Just beside Lava Rock Cafe, the General Store features great take-out pizzas.

Thai Thai Restaurant (no, that's not a misprint; that's the name) is my favorite. In fact, it's the best Thai food I've ever had! It's a bit pricy; expect to pay about $18.00 for an entrée, but it's worth it if you can afford it. Every single thing on the menu is great, but I especially love the Massaman curry. Be sure and take care that you order the seasoning the way you like it; spicy is spicy here! I always order "moderately spicy." The number is 967-7969. You can order take-out but they don't take reservations. They are open for lunch and dinner; they have lunch specials also. The beautiful Thai lady who owns this restaurant is the essence of Thai graciousness.

The Ohelo Cafe, a bit pricey, has steaks and that type of thing. They do have good pizzas and an extensive drink menu. The number is 808) 339-7865.

The best deal as far as "big" eateries in the Village is the Eagles Lighthouse Cafe. (You can ask them about the name—we don't have a lot of eagles of lighthouses in Hawaii). Just around the corner from the Upper Store, it has outdoor seating only, which is sometimes a bit drafty for our typically rainy days. However, the food is great, and again, huge portions. They serve their own homemade bread and homegrown veggies, and their sandwiches must be the biggest in the world. Two people easily fill up on one sandwich. The potato salad is the best I have had, anywhere! Ever had breadfruit salad? Ask if they have it—it's seasonal. But oh so yummy. You will probably need to adjust your belt. They also have mouth-watering desserts—try the cheesecake. You can get take-out. The number is 985-8587. They close around five or so in the evening, but they are open early for breakfast.

Outside of the Village and inside of the Park, you can eat at Kilauea Military Camp. They have a snack shop, a cafeteria, and the Lava Lounge. I guess they try, but I can't say the food is really great. Just being honest! No reservations needed!

You can also eat at the restaurant at Volcano House. Go before sunset for the great view over the caldera.

All of these eateries, with the exception of the Golf Course and Kilauea Military Camp, are conveniently located on Old Volcano Road, our "Main Street."

If you should decide you want to put down roots here—because magic happens—Allan Kroll is a well-respected realtor, as well as a notary public. His number is 967-7187. Another local realtor is Ronald Rigg. His number is 961-5255.

Well, that's about it. Volcano Village is not the Big Apple or Paris, but it is the most magical place on Earth!

In my opinion, of course.

Check out WWW.VolcanoVillageHawaii.com for great information on the Village.

Mahalo!

Mahalo nui, thank you very much, for reading my guide. I truly hope you have a most wonderful time visiting Kilauea, this very special place on our planet, and I hope you get to come again. Maybe I'll see you on the trail!

Aloha!

***

Other works by Uldra Johnson:

Bones of Love, Stories of Old Hawaii

The Insider's Guide to the Best Beaches of the Big Island

Hula Angel

and coming soon…
The Cry Room